ESSENTIALS OF

NEW LIFE

Francis M. Cosgrove, Jr.

NAVPRESS
A MINISTRY OF THE NAVIGATORS
P.O. Box 6000, Colorado Springs, Colorado 80934

The Navigators is an international, evangelical Christian organization. Jesus Christ gave His followers the Great Commission to go and make disciples (Matthew 28:19). The aim of The Navigators is to help fulfill that commission by multiplying laborers for Christ in every nation.

NavPress is the publishing ministry of The Navigators. NavPress publications are tools to help Christians grow. Although publications alone cannot make disciples or change lives, they can help believers learn biblical discipleship, and apply what they learn to their lives and ministries.

© 1978 by The Navigators
All rights reserved, including
    translation
Library of Congress Catalog Card
    Number: 78-054949
ISBN: 0-89109-427-X
14274/450
Sixth printing, 1981

Printed in the United States of
    America

CONTENTS

ILLUSTRATIONS

Dedicated to my Lord,
whose I am and whom I serve.
And to my wife, Norma,
who has co-labored with me
in disciplemaking.

AUTHOR

Francis Cosgrove is Director of Church Relations for The Navigators in Colorado Springs, Colorado. When he wrote *Essentials of New Life*, he was serving as a representative of The Navigators in Fort Lauderdale, Florida, where he was also Director of New Life at Coral Ridge Presbyterian Church.

A native of New Orleans, where he met Christ as Saviour while in high school, he came in contact with The Navigators while in the Navy. He was ordained into the ministry in 1955, and served as pastor of two churches in Colorado.

During their 20 years on Navigator staff, Francis and his wife, Norma, established new ministries in Florida at Fort Lauderdale, Jacksonville, Miami, and an Air Force base. They have also served in a U.S. military ministry in Japan and in military and collegiate ministries in San Antonio, Texas and Charleston, South Carolina.

The Cosgroves have two children, Jane and Rodney.

FOREWORD

How often I have heard the cry, "What shall we do about follow-up?" and also the lament, "There's just not enough good follow-up material around." Francis Cosgrove, who has had many years' experience with The Navigators and for some time has been Director of New Life at our church, answers both of those questions in this book.

Numerous members of our church have had their spiritual lives strengthened by the material contained in this book. The principles are not only biblical but they are preeminently practical. Many have said that for the first time they have been able to establish a daily devotional life. These classes have been taught in our church for several years and have been instrumental in establishing many new converts in the faith, and enabling them to go on and become mature and reproducing Christians.

I believe that any church which would adopt the plan of leading new Christians through this series of instruction will find that they will have better informed and more committed and zealous believers in their church.

It is a pleasure for me to recommend this book to the Christian public.

Dr. D. James Kennedy
Coral Ridge Presbyterian Church
Fort Lauderdale, Florida

PREFACE

Birth should always be followed by growth. If it isn't, something is wrong. With proper nourishment, rest, and exercise, we expect babies to grow up as normal children. Without these factors, we know their growth will be hindered, perhaps tragically.

The same is true in the spiritual realm. When men and women come to Jesus Christ—receiving Him as their personal Saviour and Lord—they are born again. As newborn babes, they need to grow. If they don't, spiritual abnormalities and tragedies result. But how do they grow up to become fruitful, productive Christians who are active in their local churches?

This question bothered me for years. I had learned the principles of follow-up and helping young Christians grow in my work with The Navigators. I had applied these while working with servicemen in Florida and Japan. But how could I best do this in a church context? How could I help our evangelists do a better job of conserving the fruits of evangelism? How could I, as a Navigator staff man, step in and assist each evangelist in the church outreach program to follow up his or her converts to Christ?

As I reflected over the training and procedures used in churches to help new Christians grow and as I studied statistics, there seemed to be no answer to the problem. I studied books and articles on follow-up, consulted with other Navigator staff, and spent much time in prayer and heart-searching. But there still were many people making professions of faith who did not become vitally involved in the local church.

While studying the Book of Acts, I stumbled across this statement, "They [the new Christians] devoted themselves to the apostles' teaching and to the fellowship, to the breaking of bread and to prayer" (Acts 2:42). Here was my answer! The key to the success of the Early Church was that the new converts were brought together under the *teaching ministry* of the apostles. These new believers, who had come to Christ on the Day of Pentecost, were being taught what was involved in living the Christian life, how to be victorious over sin, how to pray, what doctrines to believe, and the importance of a challenging, informative fellowship.

It came to me that new believers needed to *know* certain things. Yes, it is necessary for them to begin reading their Bibles, studying the Word of God, and memorizing Scripture, but they also needed to know why they are doing what their counselors told them to do. So we began a class especially designed for new Christians to help them observe and learn what was involved in living for Jesus Christ.

But what should we teach them? What was the "apostles' teaching"? My experience with The Navigators in military and collegiate ministries helped me formulate what these classes should include. After charting the necessities, we scheduled eight classes. Each one was based on topical Bible Studies I had done over the years. From these studies an outline for each class emerged. I felt these were the things a new babe in Christ needed to know.

I am now firmly convinced that most of us involved in follow-up work often expect too much performance from new believers. When we look at the earliest physical life of a child, we find that his performance is low, while input from a loving, caring parent is high. So we designed our classes in such a way that new Christians would not be overwhelmed by what they were learning, but would be able to understand what was being taught, and to realize its importance.

New converts need to *learn* a number of things rather than being asked to *do* many things. In our follow-up program, we get new believers started in reading, memorizing, and studying the Scripture immediately, but they usually don't begin doing these things consistently till hearing the session on "How to Go About Learning Bible Truths" (Chapter 3).

The results have been gratifying. I have taught the class many times now, starting over every eight weeks. Hundreds have completed all eight sessions and are continuing to grow in the faith. The vast majority of these have become actively involved in the church.

Since our church regularly holds clinics for ministers and laymen in Evangelism Explosion, many of these men have visited this class during their time with us. This book is the result of their requests for copies of my teaching outlines and the brief outlines we give to our new believers. Many churches are now successfully using this material. A leader's guide is available to enhance its usefulness.

In closing, let me offer a suggestion. We have learned that the material in this book is best presented in consecutive order, with the new converts attending all eight sessions rather than letting newcomers into the group at any time. New Christians can best be helped by waiting til the next group starts.

I want to express my appreciation to Mrs. Jean Murray for her faithful typing and transcription of the tapes from the classes. Her spirit of encouragement and cooperation has motivated me to push ahead and make this material available to churches and Christians everywhere.

FRANCIS M. COSGROVE, JR.

CHAPTER

1

KNOWING
YOU
HAVE
ETERNAL
LIFE

The Christian life begins when a person meets Jesus Christ through the Word of God and the ministry of the Holy Spirit, and personally receives Him as Saviour and Lord. You may have done that recently or quite some time ago.

Your spiritual birth can be compared to your physical birth. After you were born, you began receiving nourishment and proper care. You continued to grow till you reached physical maturity during your teen years, gained basic mental maturity in your early 20s, and matured in character during your middle or late 20s. In the same way, after you are born spiritually, you are expected to grow and mature.

The Word of God—the Bible—not only shows us how to have a relationship with God through Jesus Christ, but also challenges us to grow in our Christian lives. The Apostle Peter exhorted a group of young Christians to "grow in the grace and knowledge of our Lord and Saviour Jesus Christ" (2 Peter 3:18). The Apostle Paul, addressing the leaders of the church in ancient Ephesus, declared, "I commit you to God and to the Word of His grace, which can build you up and give you an inheritance among all those who are sanctified" (Acts 20:32). These admonitions clearly show that spiritual growth is an expected by-product of spiritual birth.

That's why we can compare spiritual growth to physical growth. When a child is born into a family, the parents' desire is to see the baby develop and begin to experience some of the wonderful things that are part of life.

Many of you can cite the specific time in your life that you can call your spiritual birthday—the day you received Jesus Christ as your Saviour and Lord. On that day you were "born again," and that by the Word of God which lives and abides forever. This is also called "conversion," and has happened in the life of every person who has received Christ as Saviour and Lord. After that new birth, growth must follow. And growth comes only as the result of applying certain basic rules.

What is necessary, then, for us to grow spiritually? What does it take to grow physically? For physical growth we need food, rest, exercise, good clean air, and some other necessary ingredients. The same is true for spiritual growth. One of the most important things we need in our Christian lives is spiritual food—the Word of God. We grow spiritually by getting to know God.

Everything we need to know about the Christian life is in the Bible. Everything we need to know about Jesus Christ, everything we need to know about the Father, everything we need to know about the Holy Spirit is in the Bible. That's how we get to know God. Some 4,000 years ago, Job recognized the importance of God's Word when he said, "I have treasured the words of His mouth more than my necessary food" (Job 23:12).

So in order to grow, we need to master the Word of God. We must take time every day to bite off a little bit, since spiritual growth takes place as we read and apply God's Word to our lives. Two basics of Christian growth taught in the Bible are knowing God's plan of salvation and having the assurance of salvation.

GOD'S PLAN OF SALVATION

The first important basic in Christian growth is to understand the Gospel clearly. We need to look at the Gospel point by point in order to know what has taken place in our lives. The Gospel—the Good News of salvation in Jesus Christ—never grows old. It bears repeating. The truth of the Gospel of Jesus Christ is, in fact, a new story every time it is told.

One night I was out calling in the Evangelism Explosion program of our church. As I shared the Gospel with a young couple, I saw again the wonderful fact that the Gospel is the power of God unto salvation, as both of them received Christ as Saviour and Lord.

Another afternoon, I had the privilege of leading a man to Christ in my office. He had come to participate in our Clinic on Evangelism and to learn how to share his faith with others. As the Gospel was presented, he discovered that he was not sure whether he knew Jesus Christ personally. I had the great joy of explaining the facts of the Gospel to him. Through the repetition of the Gospel, this man recognized his need of salvation and came to Christ.

The reason for reviewing God's plan of salvation is to clarify it in our minds, and to assure us that we are truly children of God and that Jesus Christ is in our lives.

15

What Is the Gospel?

The Apostle Paul, in one of the most doctrinally strategic books of the New Testament, wrote, "I am not ashamed of the Gospel, because it is the power of God for the salvation of everyone who believes: first for the Jew, then for the Gentile" (Romans 1:16). Paul said that the Gospel is the power of God for the salvation of any person, and that he shared this message with the world. He wrote to another church, "For what I received I passed on to you as of first importance: that Christ died for our sins according to the Scriptures, that He was buried, that He was raised on the third day according to the Scriptures" (1 Corinthians 15:3-4).

What is the Gospel? Paul tells us that the message he preached to everyone was that Jesus Christ died, was buried, and was raised again for the sins of men. Note carefully what he wrote: Jesus Christ died for our sins. The fact that Jesus Christ died is not in itself unique; everyone dies sooner or later. But Christ died for a specific reason. He died *for our sins!*

Have you recognized the fact that when Christ hung on the cross, dying, He was your substitute? He was your sin-bearer. He was taking on Himself the punishment that you deserve for your sins. He was taking your place, your hell, your judgment, and your separation from God on Himself on that cross. He died *for your sins!* Then He was buried. But on the third day He was resurrected as the sign that His death was acceptable to God.

What is the Gospel? The word *gospel* means "Good News." Good news of what? It's the Good News that Jesus Christ died on the cross for our sins, that He was buried, and that He is alive today to prove that He really brought us salvation. He has secured a place for us in heaven, and He offers us salvation as a free gift. That's the Good News.

We come to know the facts about Jesus Christ, respond to them, and receive Him as our personal Saviour and Lord—all through the Gospel, the Good News of God's salvation.

What Are the Essential Elements of the Gospel?

When we present the Gospel to other people, what do we share with them? We present to them the same set of facts from the Scriptures that were presented to us when we received Jesus Christ as Saviour and Lord.

The fact of sin. The first fact everyone needs to know is that all men are sinners. Someone once said, "You have to get a man lost before you can get him saved." Many people today do not know or believe that they are lost—separated totally and eternally from God. They do not believe that they are outside of Jesus Christ; they do not believe that they are going down the broad road to destruction. Multitudes today do not see themselves as God sees them. They do not realize that God sees people who are apart from Jesus Christ as sinners, and that the Bible clearly demonstrates the fact of sin in the human race.

The Apostle Paul stated clearly, "All have sinned and fall short of the glory of God" (Romans 3:23). That brief statement means that not one single person who ever lived, or who is living today, has reached or can reach the standard God has set. We all come short of it. We are all sinners by nature. Everything we do and every direction in which we go is always toward sin. Why does a little child have temper tantrums and ram his head against a wall? Because he can't have his own way, and his will goes in the direction of sin and disobedience. Man is a sinner by nature.

We are also sinners by choice. An Old Testament

17

prophet graphically portrayed us this way: "All of us like sheep have gone astray; we have turned everyone to his own way" (Isaiah 53:6). Each of us has turned *to his own way*. This means we have deliberately done things we know are wrong. Dr. D. James Kennedy, senior minister of Coral Ridge Presbyterian Church, Fort Lauderdale, Florida, has said that when he travels around the world he usually asks one basic question of any person he meets: "Do you always live up to what you know is right, and have you always done that?" The answer is always the same. First, people laugh. Then they reply, "Of course not. I don't always live up to what I know is right."

That answer is international, trans-cultural, and transcends all religions. Whether the person is a Hindu, a Buddhist, a Muslim, a Jew, a nominal Christian, or of any other religion, the answer is always the same—a laugh and a denial of being able to live up to what he knows is right. That universal admission illustrates the fact that all men are sinners by choice. We know what the right standard is, but we go against our consciences and do what is wrong. The Apostle Paul wrote, "The Scripture declares that the whole world is a prisoner of sin" (Galatians 3:22). That is the fact of sin.

The penalty of sin. The Bible not only confronts us with the fact of sin, it also states there is a death penalty attached to sin. "The wages of sin is death," Paul declared, "but the gift of God is eternal life through Christ Jesus our Lord" (Romans 6:23). The contrast is tremendous. On one side we have the awful wages of sin; on the other, the marvelous gift of God—eternal life through Jesus Christ. On one side is the death penalty; on the other are freedom and eternal life through Christ. The death sentence is the penalty of sin, as Paul explains in another statement: "Therefore, just as sin entered the world through one man, and death through sin, and in this way death came to all men, because all sinned" (Romans 5:12).

When the Bible says the penalty of sin is death, it means spiritual death. Adam and Eve, the first human sinners and the ancestors of all mankind, died spiritually when they disobeyed God. They had been told not to eat of the tree of the knowledge of good and evil (see Genesis 2:17), but they ate the fruit anyway (see Genesis 3:6). One result of this sin was that they died spiritually.

Paul said, "As for you, you were dead in your transgressions and sins" (Ephesians 2:1). That is the spiritual condition of every person outside of Christ. What can a dead person do? Nothing! The Bible tells us that a person without Jesus Christ is dead and therefore cannot hear or see. He is spiritually lifeless. Unless God in His mercy opens our eyes, unplugs our ears, and gives us life, we will never see God in heaven. Paul describes this eternal separation vividly: "He will punish those who do not know God and do not obey the Gospel of our Lord Jesus. They will be punished with everlasting destruction and shut out from the presence of the Lord and from the majesty of His power" (2 Thessalonians 1:8-9).

Sin's penalty must be paid. Another strategic, all-important point is made by the writer to the Hebrews: "Man is destined to die once, and after that to face judgment" (Hebrews 9:27). Note the sequence here: After death comes judgment. Just as men are destined to die, they are destined to stand judgment. No one escapes death; all of us will certainly die someday. After death we face judgment—just as certain and sure.

What happens at judgment? That's when everyone will face God the Judge, and He will punish sin and make everything right. Everything hidden over the years is going to come out. Everything said in secret will be shouted from

19

the rooftops. Nothing done, said, or even thought will be hidden, but will be brought out into the open and judged by God. The penalty of our sins must be paid, and will be. Because of who God is, He cannot excuse our sins and just say, "Oh, I'll forget them." Because He is the holy and righteous God, He has to deal with them.

In our Evangelism Explosion program, we learn a beautiful illustration to share the fact that God will not excuse our sins or simply forget them. Let's suppose I were to rob a bank of $5,000, and during the robbery the teller, a number of customers, and the TV camera were to identify me clearly. I manage to get away, but am arrested shortly afterward, and in due process am brought before a judge. All the evidence before the court clearly shows that I am the culprit.

The judge passes sentence, and as I am about to be led away I turn to him and make this promise: "Your Honor, no one was hurt in the robbery; all the money has been returned. If you let me go, I promise never to rob another bank again." Now the question is this: Would the judge be just if he let me go? No, because he has a standard of justice he must maintain. Also, no bank in the land would be safe if criminals were allowed to go free if they said they were sorry and promised to rob no more banks.

When you consider this, remember God is a more just Judge than any human jurist. He cannot simply excuse our sins and forget about them because we say we are sorry and promise never to commit sins again.

Christ paid the penalty of sin. God, however, had a plan to get us out of this hopeless and helpless situation. "But God demonstrates His own love for us in this: While we were still sinners, Christ died for us" (Romans 5:8). Note the tremendous significance of this statement: God demonstrated His love toward us—showed it visibly—

while we were still sinners. He did not wait for us to get better. Even though we were His enemies, representing everything that was repulsive to Him, God loved us so much that He sent His Son into the world to take that penalty on Himself at Calvary.

He hung on the cross as our substitute, dying a horrible death so the penalty of our sins might be paid. That is the heart of the Gospel. It is important for us to go over it again and again to see all of its meaning.

Paul also stated, "God made Him [Jesus Christ] who had no sin to be sin for us, so that in Him we might become the righteousness of God" (2 Corinthians 5:21). In this profound statement, Paul is saying that when Jesus hung on the cross, crying out, "My God, My God, why have You forsaken Me?" (Matthew 27:46), at that moment of history He was taking all our sins on Himself. This was such a dreadful thing that Jesus felt the awful anguish of having God the Father turn His back on Him, His own Son.

The very words Jesus uttered were a fulfillment of an Old Testament prophecy: "My God, My God, why hast Thou forsaken Me?" (Psalm 22:1) God had planned the payment of the penalty of sin from antiquity. Jesus said, "For God so loved the world that He gave His one and only Son, that whoever believes in Him shall not perish but have everlasting life" (John 3:16).

Most people today trust in their own good works for salvation, hoping to offer them to God as their entry permit into heaven. In answer to God's potential question, "Why should I let you into My heaven?" they show their good works and say in effect, "Lord, take these. I don't care what You did on the cross. You'd better accept these and let me in!"

But the Scripture is very clear about what God is going to say to those who refuse Christ's payment of the penalty of sin: "I never knew you. Away from Me, you evildoers!" (Matthew 7:23)

Dr. Kennedy estimates that 95% of American church members have no idea what it is to know that they have eternal life only through the merits of Jesus Christ. Along with most people around the world, they are trusting in their own efforts. The ancient prophet stated, "For all of us have become like one who is unclean, and all our righteous deeds are like a filthy garment; and all of us wither like a leaf, and our iniquities, like the wind, take us away" (Isaiah 64:6).

Pick up your Bible and suppose that it is the record book of your life. You open it to page one and find on it your name and all the necessary vital statistics. As you begin to fan through the pages of this book, you discover that God has recorded everything you've ever done. Every good thing you've ever done is written down, but also every bad thing. Every sin you have committed is recorded whether it be in thought, word, or deed, whether by commission (what you did on purpose) or omission (the good you should have done but didn't). The pages are heavy-laden with your wrongdoings.

When you realize what is in this book, you also realize that this weight of sin is on you. Visualize this by placing the book on your right hand, which represents you. So now the whole weight of it is on you. Consider your left hand as Jesus Christ, and listen to what the Bible has to say: "All of us like sheep have gone astray, each of us has turned to his own way; but the Lord has caused the iniquity of us all to fall on Him [Jesus Christ]" (Isaiah 53:6). That is, God has taken the sins that weigh on us and has placed them on Jesus Christ. (Transfer the book you are holding with your right hand to the left. Your right hand—you—is now free from the weight of the book—sin.)

Jesus Christ, dying as our substitute, "Himself bore our sins in His body on the cross" (1 Peter 2:24). He paid the supreme penalty for all our sins. When He had done so, He cried out, "It is finished" (John 19:30). The term used here is *tetelestai*, a Greek commercial term meaning "paid in full." Jesus Christ has paid in full for all our sins, providing us a heavenly home.

Salvation is a free gift. Salvation is not something we can earn or deserve. God gives salvation and eternal life to us *freely.* They don't cost us anything; we can't work for them; we receive them only through God's grace. The Apostle Paul said, "It is by grace you have been saved, through faith—and this not from yourselves, it is the gift of God—not by works, so that no one can boast" (Ephesians 2:8-9). "He saved us, not because of righteous things we had done, but because of His mercy. He saved us through the washing of rebirth and renewal by the Holy Spirit, whom He poured out on us generously through Jesus Christ our Saviour, so that, having been justified by His grace, we might become heirs having the hope of eternal life" (Titus 3:5-7). Salvation and eternal life are a free gift.

King David, an Old Testament psalm writer, said, "He brought me up out of the pit of destruction, out of the miry clay; and He set my feet upon a rock making my footsteps firm. And He put a new song in my mouth, a song of praise to our God; many will see and fear, and will trust in the Lord" (Psalm 40:2-3). God has done it all. All we can say is, "Thank You, Lord. I know it wasn't my doing. It's all You; You have done it. Thank You!"

We must receive Jesus Christ. This last step is vital. We must receive Jesus Christ into our lives personally. We can understand all the facts. We can understand and even acknowledge that we are sinners, that a death penalty is hanging over our heads, that a judgment is coming, that Jesus Christ died for us, and that salvation is a free gift. But unless we open our hearts and let Jesus Christ in as Saviour and Lord, we still don't have His salvation. We are still in our sins and under God's judgment.

Jesus Himself said, "Here I am! I stand at the door and knock. If anyone hears My voice and opens the door, I will go in and eat with him, and he with Me" (Revelation 3:20). Jesus says that we need to reach down and open the doors of our lives and invite Him to come into our lives as He said He would. John wrote, "To all who received Him, to those who believed in His name, He gave the right to become children of God" (John 1:12). We must receive Him.

Then we can answer God's potential question with: "You should let me into Your heaven because Jesus Christ died on the cross for my sins."

The Assurance of Salvation

When I was 17, I invited Jesus Christ to come into my life. I remember that decision clearly. But it was another two years, after I enlisted in the Navy, before I came to an assurance of my salvation. No one in the church where I met Christ had sat down with me and shown me from the Bible that I could know I have eternal life. I knew Jesus Christ had come into my life; I knew my life had changed. I saw all kinds of evidences of my new life, but down in my heart I was still not sure. God eventually used another sailor to show me from the Scriptures how I could know that I have eternal life.

We can have assurance of salvation, that is, we can *know* we have eternal life for these six reasons:

God Says So

The Apostle John stated, "I write these things to you who believe in the name of the Son of God so that you may know that you have eternal life" (1 John 5:13). We know we have eternal life because God says so in His Word.

Many people make the mistake of basing the certainty of their relationship to God on their feelings. Now we don't want to question the fact that when a person receives Christ's gift of salvation some great feelings accompany that transaction. The burdens are lifted, a new joy comes in, spiritual eyes are opened, ears can now hear, and the mind can understand spiritual truth, and many things can be seen from God's point of view. But feelings can be misleading, for there are times in our lives when we just don't *feel* we are Christians.

I have been a Christian for many years, but some days I feel like I am going to hell for sure. On other days, when everything is going fine, I feel that I'm going to heaven. But my assurance is not to be based on my feelings because the devil is constantly working on them. We know we have passed from death to life because God Himself has said so, and we simply need to take Him at His word.

Both young Christians and older Christians, if they are not already doing it, need to get into the Word of God for themselves. It is the Bible that tells us we can know we have eternal life: "And this is the testimony: God has given us eternal life, and this life is in His Son. He who has the Son has life; he who does not have the Son of God does not have life" (1 John 5:11-12).

When the Korean War broke out and the Army went after me, I joined the Navy, not wanting to be in the mud and filth of the ground war in Korea. I'd been a Christian for less than two years, and everything was fine as long as I was around friends at church and in the worship services. I knew that Jesus Christ had entered my life, but that was about all. When I was first exposed to Navy life, however, I degenerated into dreadful spiritual condition.

I found myself living with the kind of crude, worldly men I had never associated with in civilian life. I had avoided such men, but now they were all around me. I tried to witness to some of them, but all I did was get into arguments. My witness was not honoring to God, but I didn't know any better. My spiritual life degenerated because I didn't know I had eternal life; my assurance rested on nothing more than my feelings. And most of the time, surrounded by these men, I didn't feel very good.

Then I met a Christian sailor who introduced me to Bible study, Scripture memory, and other means by which I could begin growing spiritually. Through the Bible I gained assurance of my salvation. (In the next chapter we will consider the importance of the Bible in our lives.) I discovered—through my new friend and other Christians to whom he introduced me—that I was starving to death spiritually and didn't know it.

No one had told me the Bible was food for my soul. No one had shown me how I should take in the Word of God for myself. No one had explained to me how the Bible could give me assurance of salvation.

How do we know we have eternal life? Because God says so in the Scriptures. It's that cut and dried, that simple. If you have received Jesus Christ as your Saviour and Lord, then the Bible says you have eternal life. You can be sure of it. Why? Because God says so.

During His ministry, Jesus stated, "I tell you the truth, whoever hears My word and believes Him who sent Me has eternal life and will not be condemned; he has crossed over from death to life" (John 5:24). When Jesus wanted to make an emphatic statement to those to whom He was ministering, He often prefaced it by saying, "I tell you the truth" ("Verily, verily" in the *King James Version*). He emphasizes here that the person who believes in Him possesses eternal life as a permanent feature of his life.

On two other occasions Jesus repeated this truth: "I tell you the truth, he who believes has everlasting life" (John 6:47); "My sheep listen to My voice; I know them, and they follow Me. I give them eternal life, and they shall never perish; no one can snatch them out of My hand. My Father, who has given them to Me, is greater than all; no one can snatch them out of My Father's hand" (John 10:27-29). Jesus said, "My sheep" (those who belong to Him) are those who "hear My voice" (those who have responded to Him). Those who have received Jesus Christ as Saviour and Lord (those who have believed in Him) are secure in the His hand. Christ, furthermore, is secure in the Father's hand. So we have double security! That is the promise of Scripture. We can know we have eternal life because God has said so in His Word.

God's Spirit Testifies with Our Spirits that We Are God's Children

The second reason we can know we have eternal life is because of the ministry of the Holy Spirit of God within us. Paul tells us, "The Spirit Himself testifies with our spirit that we are God's children. Now if we are children, then we are heirs—heirs of God and co-heirs with Christ, if indeed we share in His sufferings in order that we may also share in His glory" (Romans 8:16-17).

When we become Christians, a new rapport is formed between God's Holy Spirit and our spirits. He comes to live in us. Every believer has the Spirit of God residing in his heart. His presence is one of the benefits of our salvation. He is there to make us sensitive to sin; He is within us to lead us in the right paths; He opens the Scriptures to us so we can understand them; and He makes His presence known to us in many ways.

One of the Spirit's major responsibilities is to testify to us that we are God's children.

Changes Have Taken Place in Our Lives

The third way in which we can know we have eternal life is through the changes taking place in our lives. Have you experienced changes since you became a Christian? Has there been a change in your thinking, in your habits, in your overall life? Paul declared, "Therefore, if anyone is in Christ, he is a new creation; the old has gone, the new has come!" (2 Corinthians 5:17)

Over 25 years ago, I knew immediately after receiving Christ that my life had changed. One of the reasons I had that assurance was that the Bible had suddenly become precious to me. This is one of the evidences we have of possessing eternal life—we want to explore this Book that God gave us. We just can't get enough of it. We have a great hunger for it.

A man once came to our church offices who had experienced a crisis a few days before. In turmoil he had flown to Niagara Falls, New York, where he met a friend who shared Christ with him. His friend told him to come to our church for further help, so he flew to Fort Lauderdale. My secretary talked with him, gave him a Bible study and Scripture memory booklet called *Knowing Christ*,[1] and made an appointment for him to see me the next day.

When he came back the following morning, he had read all of John's Gospel, had memorized all four verses in the booklet, and had done both of the Bible studies in *Knowing Christ*. This was clear evidence that this man really had come to know Jesus Christ—he had a hunger for God's Word.

We may not understand everything in the Bible, but we go on reading it daily. We realize that Scripture is the source of everything in our new relationship with God, and we want to know Him through it. We may say, "Lord, I know this is Your Word, and I know that I can't understand much of it yet. But I can understand what You want me to, so I'm going to continue getting to know You through it." The more we read, the more exhilarated and challenged we become. And as the Word is increasingly assimilated into our lives, more changes will occur and we will understand more of it.

We also see changes in our outlook on life, our attitudes toward people, and our relationships with people. As Christians we can see things from God's point of view, and we see history, events in the world, and life around us from a new perspective.

We begin getting along with people whom we previously disliked or even hated. We can see them through the eyes of Christ. Our relationships with others—husbands, wives, parents, children, employers, employees—also begin improving as we begin following biblical principles for getting along one with another.

If you are still the same old self, and nothing has changed in all the many facets of your life, you should evaluate whether you have received Jesus Christ as your personal Saviour and Lord, since a major evidence that you have eternal life is the changes that have taken place in your life.

We Love Our Brothers and Sisters in Christ

The fourth reason for knowing we have eternal life is that we now love our brothers and sisters in the Lord.

That's the way the Bible words it: "We know that we have passed from death to life, because we love our brothers. Anyone who does not love remains in death" (1 John 3:14).

We love our fellow Christians. We want to be around them; we want their fellowship; we want their encouragement; we want to do things for them. Our prejudices have changed to acceptance; our hatreds have turned to love. We now love our brothers and sisters in Christ.

As I have traveled around the world, I've had an immediate rapport with Christians. I may not have been able to understand a word of their language or they of mine, but there was a love between us. I could understand, recognize, and communicate basic things—primarily that I knew Jesus Christ as they did. Although I could not converse with these believers, I could worship with them and even hum their songs. I knew what they were saying and singing. We were brethren together.

When God gave us eternal life, he gave us a desire for His people, and our attitudes toward fellow believers changed. So we must ask ourselves this question: Do we enjoy being around other Christians? We can know we have eternal life because we love other believers and enjoy being around them.

We Want to Share the Saviour with Others

Another evidence that we have eternal life is that we want our relatives and friends to know Jesus Christ. When I first came to the Lord, almost immediately I thought of my father, my mother, my brothers and sisters, and my friends. I wanted them to know my Saviour. I wanted them to experience what I had experienced.

This great desire has never left me. When I entered the Navy, I was surrounded by multitudes of men who couldn't care less about God, but there was always that strong desire to communicate to them the Good News that they could have salvation in Christ. After I had finally received some training and had memorized a few verses of Scripture, I could share that Gospel intelligently.

When you meet a stranger, what is the first thought that goes through your mind? Do you wonder if that person knows the Saviour?

I don't have to remind myself to wonder if he or she knows Jesus. By now it is an instantaneous response. Instinctively I am concerned for that person. I wonder if he or she knows Jesus Christ.

Are you like that? This is not a judgment you pass, but rather a discernment on your part. Discernment is a necessary part of your desire to help others know your Saviour. If you know Christ, you will want others to know Him as well. If you don't have this desire for the people around you, then something is wrong with your relationship with Jesus.

In one of his letters, Paul said, "The Lord's message rang out from you not only in Macedonia and Achaia—your faith in God has become known everywhere. Therefore we do not need to say anything about it, for they themselves report what kind of reception you gave us. They tell how you turned to God from idols to serve the living and true God" (1 Thessalonians 1:8-9). Paul was stating a simple fact: Those who had received Christ as Saviour and Lord in Thessalonica were now declaring that Good News in their city and in the surrounding areas.

Evangelism is a command of Christ, and all Christians are to be involved in it. Our desire to share Jesus with others is an evidence that He is in us and that we have eternal life.

We Want to Live Godly Lives

The sixth evidence that we have eternal life is that we want to be pure and free from sin—the desire to live godly lives. A person cannot claim to have received Jesus Christ as Saviour and Lord and then continue to live in sin and practice it. True repentance will always be seen in the life of a Christian by a change of lifestyle. When the Holy Spirit enters our lives and takes up residence in our hearts, He begins to make us sensitive to sin. Habits and practices that are sinful begin to leave.

I once talked with a young woman in my office who suddenly broke down and began to cry. She was deeply concerned about her spiritual life. It was wrong biblically for her to live with a man to whom she was not married. She knew that as a Christian the affair had to stop.

Purity must characterize the life of the Christian. John wrote, "Everyone who has this hope [of Christ's second coming] in him purifies himself, just as He [God] is pure. Everyone who sins breaks the law; in fact, sin is lawlessness. But you know that He appeared so that He might take away our sins. And in Him is no sin. No one who lives in Him keeps on sinning. No one who continues to sin has either seen Him or known Him. Dear children, do not let anyone lead you astray. He who does what is right is righteous, just as He is righteous" (1 John 3:3-7).

Only through the grace of God can we be pure. Paul wrote, "For the grace of God that brings salvation has appeared to all men. It teaches us to say 'No' to ungodliness and worldly passions, and to live self-controlled, upright and godly lives in this present age" (Titus 2:11-12).

If we claim to have received Christ as Saviour and Lord and continue to live in sin, we are only deceiving ourselves. Every part of us—our work, our habits, our friendships, our relationships—has to come under the searchlight of God. An important evidence of eternal life is the desire to live righteously.

* * *

How can we know that we have eternal life? We have looked at six evidences:

1. God says so.
2. God's Spirit testifies with our spirits that we are God's children.
3. Changes have taken place in our lives.
4. We love our brothers and sisters in Christ.
5. We want to share the Saviour with others.
6. We want to live godly lives.

The Bible commands us to make our calling and election sure (see 2 Peter 1:10). It also tells us to examine ourselves to see whether we are in the faith (see 2 Corinthians 13:5). Throughout history the Church's strength has been that all true Christians *knew* they had eternal life.

As you evaluate your life in light of the above six evidences, can you honestly say, "I know that I have eternal life because all of these evidences are present in my life"? If not, then perhaps your lack of assurance is simply because Jesus Christ is not in your life. That you can change by receiving Him as your personal Saviour and Lord right now.

Jesus said, "Whoever comes to Me I will never drive away" (John 6:37).

NOTE: 1. Available from the Follow-up Department, The Billy Graham Association, Box 779, Minneapolis, Minnesota 55440.

CHAPTER

2

THE
IMPORTANCE
OF THE
BIBLE IN
DAILY LIFE

When a man is about to die, he is not too concerned about trivial and insignificant things. He is concerned with the fundamentals of life that make a real difference.

Shortly before his death, the Apostle Paul wrote these words to Timothy, a man with whom he had spent a number of years: "But as for you, continue in what you have learned and have become convinced of, because you know those from whom you learned it" (2 Timothy 3:14). One of "those" to whom he was referring was his own ministry in Timothy's life. Paul continued: "And how from infancy you have known the holy Scriptures, which are able to make you wise for salvation through faith in Christ Jesus. All Scripture is God-breathed and is useful for teaching, rebuking, correcting and training in righteousness, so that the man of God may be thoroughly equipped for every good work" (2 Timothy 3:15-17).

An excellent paraphrase of the last part of this passage reads, "The Scriptures are the comprehensive equipment of the man of God, and fit him fully for all branches of his work"

(2 Timothy 3:17, PH). The Scriptures are comprehensive—all-inclusive. All you need to know *spiritually* is in the Bible; you don't need anything else as a Christian. The Bible also is the finest book you can find on psychology, or on a part of the history of the Near East. The Bible has much to say on many subjects and is extremely interesting.

King Solomon of Israel had much to say about how we should approach Scripture: "My son, if you will receive my sayings, and treasure my commandments within you, make your ear attentive to wisdom, incline your heart to understanding; for if you cry for discernment, lift your voice for understanding; if you seek her as silver, and search for her as for hidden treasures; then you will discern the fear of the Lord, and discover the knowledge of God" (Proverbs 2:1-5).

If we take time to look closely into God's Word, we will find the knowledge of God—we will get to know Him. We will also learn to reverence Him, to have the proper regard for Him. Notice the active verbs in this passage; they are quite striking. The first one is *receive*; then come *treasure, make attentive, incline, cry, lift, seek, search*. These all indicate action. They show desire and motion. Our deliberate reading of the Scriptures enables us to know God and to reverence Him properly.

THE HOLY BIBLE

What Book gives us the knowledge of God? The Bible. We also call it the Word of God, Scripture, the Scriptures, the Bread of Life, the Holy Bible. It comes from a holy God; it was written by holy men of God; it was given by inspiration of the Holy Spirit, who is its Divine Author; it concerns itself with holy things and was written so that we might live holy lives. It was penned by some 40 human authors from many walks of life—kings, common people, philosophers, fishermen, scholars, the uneducated, poets, farmers, statesmen, carpenters.

The Bible was written over a period of 1,500 years, originally in three languages: the Old Testament primarily in Hebrew with a small section of Aramaic, and the New Testament in Greek. But it occupies itself with one major theme—the redemption of human beings. It reveals how God provided a way that all of us might be brought into a meaningful relationship with Him.

The Bible teaches us truths we cannot learn for ourselves, and without them our lives are incomplete. Its ethical guidelines are still up-to-date. Profound, yet simple, the Bible has material in it that is satisfying to the deepest thinker and understandable to a little child. Every Christian who makes the effort to read it can understand what he has read.

The Bible's Unique Continuity

The Bible is a continuous story from the first words of the Book of Genesis to the last words of the Book of Revelation. It is truly amazing that such a large group of writers over hundreds of years could write *one* book in which all the parts fit together perfectly. The Bible's unity might be likened to assigning 40 painters a piece of a painting when they cannot consult one another; yet when the finished pieces are put together, they result in a perfectly whole picture. Only through the inspiration of the Holy Spirit was the Bible's unity possible, for He so superintended its writing that the result was a continuous whole.

The Bible's Unique Circulation

No other book in human history has been in demand as much as the Bible. Today valiant men and women are risking their lives to distribute this Book in countries where it is banned. In "free" countries, expert linguists are working diligently on translating this Book into every language of the world. Their purpose is to make it possible for the people of every nation to read God's Word for themselves, and to know the God and the Saviour revealed in its pages. To this task the Wycliffe Bible Translators have been called. They have worked feverishly to get the Bible translated into every possible tribal language. It is thrilling to read about the great celebration that occurs when a chief of some obscure Indian tribe receives the first copy of the New Testament in his tribe's own language. By God's grace and with God's help, someday the Bible will be available in every language for people to read.

The Bible's Many Translations

The Bible has been translated into about 1,300 languages, yet there are more than 3,000 others to go.

I attended a conference many years ago at which I heard Kenny Watters speak about the ministry of Bible translation. At the time, Kenny was in charge of the home office of Wycliffe Bible Translators, and he spoke on his organization's ministry. I was moved of God toward the Wycliffe style of ministry, became interested in it, and would have loved to have become part of that great team. But God led differently, and I came to work with The Navigators instead. It is interesting to note, however, that through the years The Navigators have channeled some 700 people into the Wycliffe organization. Dawson Trotman, founder and first president of The Navigators, served on the board of Wycliffe till his death in 1956.

The Bible's Unique Survival

Do we realize what a privilege we have in a free society of being able to read and study the Bible? It is easy to forget that many people have given their lives so we can have the Word of God freely available to us. Think of John Wycliffe, some 500 years ago, whom God led to translate the Scriptures into vernacular English so that the people of the British Isles could read the Word of God for themselves. He literally gave his life to that task. He was a pioneer for all subsequent English translators of the Bible, and we can all be grateful to God for his work.

Foxe's Book of Martyrs is an inspiring classic about Christian martyrs from the time of Christ to the mid-1850s. It records the experiences of countless Christians who suffered tremendous persecution in order to have the Bible printed in the language of the people. Courageous Christian printers sometimes would publish portions of the Bible, only to have the books stolen and burned in public bonfires.

In 1968 my wife and I traveled through the Middle East on our way home from Japan. We visited Palestine and stopped off to see the caves where the Dead Sea Scrolls had been discovered. I had seen pictures of these scrolls—one of the greatest discoveries of the 20th century—and had read extensively about them. When the scholars translated the Dead Sea Scrolls, they found that the Book of Isaiah (the first of the Major Prophets in the Old Testament) did not differ substantially from other translations of manuscripts that were much later than the Dead Sea Scrolls. God has seen to it that His Word has been preserved.

THE BIBLE'S CLAIMS FOR ITSELF

What does the Bible say about itself? Many things, but we will look at only five of them.

The Bible Is the Very Voice of God

The Bible is the voice of God. It is the last word on all spiritual issues. It is categorically final. What the Bible says is exactly the way life is, and we need to know, recognize, believe and live by those truths. The Bible is not an ordinary book. Jesus Christ said, "As for the person who hears My words but does not keep them, I do not judge him. For I did not come to judge the world, but to save it. There is a judge for the one who rejects Me and does not accept My words; that very word which I spoke will condemn him at the last day" (John 12:47-48). His Word will be the basis by which all men will be judged.

In the Sermon on the Mount, Jesus verified the authority of the Scripture: "I tell you the truth, until heaven and earth disappear, not the smallest letter, not the least stroke of a pen, will by any means disappear from the Law until everything is accomplished" (Matthew 5:18).

The person who has obeyed the teachings of the Bible has come to experience a rich, abundant and overflowing life. When we encounter someone like that, we can be sure he or she is living under the authority of God's Word.

The Bible Is Very Influential

The Bible produces a response in us by the very nature of its claims. The Prophet Jeremiah described the Word of God in terms of its influence: "Therefore, thus says the Lord, the God of hosts, 'Because you have spoken this word, behold, I am making My words in your mouth fire and this people wood, and it will consume them'" (Jeremiah 5:14). He also wrote, "'Is not My word like fire?' declares the Lord, 'and like a hammer which shatters a rock?'" (Jeremiah 23:29)

Fire and a hammer are influential tools. Fire has been of great benefit to man, and he uses it to shape or weld things together. Fire is also a consuming agent which destroys and devours everything in its path. The picture Jeremiah paints is clear: if we fail to heed scriptural teachings, we will find out—very often too late—that they will consume us.

The hammer, on the other hand, gives us the picture of a crushing or shaping force. So it is with the Word of God. If we fail to heed its message, it will eventually crush us.

The Bible Is Life-giving

After the departure of many of His followers, Jesus said, "The Spirit gives life; the flesh counts for nothing. The words I have spoken to you are spirit and they are life" (John 6:63). Christ's words are life-giving. We are born again "through the living and enduring Word of God" (1 Peter 1:23). No one has ever come to know and experience the new birth apart from the Word of God. The Holy Spirit can use an entire passage, a chapter, or even a verse to bring about the regeneration of a life.

We learn of our need of Christ as Saviour and Lord from the Scriptures. Through them we come to understand our sinful natures and the consequences of sin, the import of the finished work of Christ on the cross, and our need to respond and receive Him and the gift of eternal life.

The Bible Is a Sword for Battle

The Bible is both the offensive and defensive weapon for spiritual warfare. As the Apostle Paul described the Christian's armor for our spiritual battles, he spoke in terms of a Roman soldier's military equipment. Describing the various pieces of that armor and their spiritual counterparts, he said, "Take the helmet of salvation and the sword of the Spirit, which is the Word of God" (Ephesians 6:17).

The Scriptures are the sword of the Spirit. We are all engaged in a spiritual battle, and that battle requires spiritual weapons. A soldier must know not only the various weapons and their capabilities in battle, but also how to use them and keep them in operational condition. As our sword for the battle, we need to keep our knowledge and use of Scripture sharp. If we don't, its tremendous influential power to change our lives and protect us is greatly diminished.

The Bible Is a Probing Instrument

The writer of the Book of Hebrews stated, "The Word of God is living and active. Sharper than any double-edged sword, it penetrates even to dividing soul and spirit, joints and marrow; it judges the thoughts and attitudes of the heart" (Hebrews 4:12). We have all experienced the probing work of the Word of God which checks our attitudes and motives. How many times have we planned a course of action, only to find that God was not pleased with it because we were seeking self-gratification or self-exaltation? Jesus spoke of this when He said that keeping the commandments is an inward obedience, not only an outward one (see Mark 7:14-23).

THE INSPIRATION OF THE BIBLE

Our purpose here is not to go into a lengthy, detailed discussion of the absolute reliability of the Scriptures, for many learned men have written eloquently to defend them. Instead, let's look at some internal evidences from a layman's viewpoint.

Paul declared to one of his team members, "All Scripture is God-breathed and is useful for teaching, rebuking, correcting and training in righteousness" (2 Timothy 3:16). This statement begins with the phrase, "All Scripture." That means every verse of the Bible is God-breathed—not just parts of it, as some are teaching today.

None of the Scripture writers tried to explain this; they just knew what they wrote was from God. Again and again they stated, "Thus says the Lord," or "The Word of the Lord came to me"; or they recorded God saying, "I have put My words in your mouth."

The Apostle Peter wrote, "Men spoke from God as they were carried along by the Holy Spirit" (2 Peter 1:21). We didn't receive the Scriptures by the will of any man. God Himself inspired men to write every single word, and these sacred writings are absolutely trustworthy.

As we study the Word of God, we are amazed by its accuracy, as for example the order of the words in Psalm 37:3-7. In this passage, four words, all verbs, describe actions related to a relationship with God.

The first word is *trust* (verse 3). It means "to rely upon," "depend upon," or "yield to." We start with "trust in the Lord" in any experience of the Christian life.

In verse four, the verb is *delight*. It is hard to delight in someone we don't trust. The next word is *commit* (verse 5). It means "to give in sacred trust." Commit what? your way," that is, the direction of our lives. All of us know people who are apparently just existing and making little contribution to anything significant.

It is impossible to commit our lives to God unless we first trust Him and then delight in Him. The only way we can experience this trust and delight is found in verse seven. Here we find the word *rest*. It means "to repose from all anxiety." In other words, we can be sure God will show us the way we must go in life and the work we must do (see Jeremiah 42:3).

The Bible as a whole claims inspiration for itself and Jesus Christ claims it for His words. The late Dr. Addison H. Leitch, former president of Pittsburgh Xenia Theological Seminary, made this statement:

> Perhaps it [divine inspiration] was maintained but unexplained [by biblical writers] because it cannot be explained, but they all knew the difference between what they were saying under that inspiration and what they were saying apart from it. Their claims to authority are magnificent and final; our inability to define at this point should not lead us to discard the high and unique claims.[1]

Let's examine three basic truths about inspiration.

1 The Bible Is Fully Inspired

We believe in the full and complete inspiration of the Bible. We believe the creation story in Genesis as well as the miracle stories in the Gospels, the account of the virgin birth of Jesus, and the description of Noah's ark and the flood.

We believe God created the heavens and the earth—the entire universe. Isn't it amazing how easily the doctrine of evolution is perpetrated in our schools and colleges today without substantial opposition? The creationist viewpoint often is ignored. We believe in the Bible's teaching of a God-created universe because we know the Bible is fully inspired by God, who knows all answers and speaks only truth.

2 The Bible Is Verbally Inspired

God didn't just inspire the ideas of Scripture and leave it up to His writers to put them into words; He inspired the very words the writers used. One theory holds that God gave certain men great thoughts and left it up to each man's own ingenuity as to how to write them. But this theory denies that the Bible is verbally inspired, and suggests mistakes in its wording.

God said to Jeremiah, "I have put My words in your mouth" (Jeremiah 1:9), and the prophet declared, "The Word of the Lord came to me" (Jeremiah 1:4). Of the Prophet Samuel we read, "The Lord revealed Himself to Samuel at Shiloh by the Word of the Lord" (1 Samuel 3:21).

3 The Bible is Infallible

The Holy Spirit made sure that the Bible cannot fail or make mistakes. Scripture has no errors. It is the absolute truth. Since the Bible is inspired by God it has to be true. God cannot lie; He can only speak the truth.

Jesus said, "The Scripture cannot be broken" (John 10:35). Addressing the Father, He also said, "Your Word is truth" (John 17:17). Every biblical statement and prophecy is true, infallible, and authoritative.

Infallibility applies to the original manuscripts. Although transmission errors have crept into translations over the years, these errors are reconcilable. They came into the Scripture through translators and copiers, incidentally and accidentally, not intentionally.

We believe with historic Christianity that the Bible is fully and verbally inspired by God, and is infallible.

WHY DID GOD GIVE US THE BIBLE?

God gave us the Bible for many reasons. We will concentrate here on six of them.

45

| The Bible Was Given to Reveal Jesus Christ to Us

In describing the purpose for writing his Gospel, the Apostle John said, "These are written that you may believe that Jesus is the Christ, the Son of God, and that by believing you may have life in His name" (John 20:31). This statement also summarizes the entire Scriptures. We see Jesus Christ throughout both the Old and New Testaments.

The Gospels are not the only books that reveal Christ to us, for references to Him abound in other books. Consider the Book of Joshua as an example. After Joshua brought the Israelites successfully across the flooded Jordan River, which God had miraculously held back, the people camped in Gilgal near Jericho.

> Now it came about when Joshua was by Jericho, that he lifted up his eyes and looked, and behold, a man was standing opposite him with his sword drawn in his hand, and Joshua went to him and said to him, "Are you for us or for our adversaries?"
>
> And he said, "No, rather I indeed come now as captain of the host of the Lord."
>
> And Joshua fell on his face to the earth, and bowed down, and said to him, "What has my lord to say to his servant?"
>
> And the captain of the Lord's host said to Joshua, "Remove your sandals from your feet, for the place where you are standing is holy." And Joshua did so (Joshua 5:13-15).

Whom did Joshua meet? Many Bible scholars believe that he met Jesus Christ in one of His preincarnate appearances, here revealed as being in charge of the armies of God.

The Bible also records many predictions made years

46

before the prophesied event came to pass. Centuries before Jesus was born, prophets recorded hundreds of prophecies regarding His coming. The detail of the predictions and the exact fulfillment of each one is overwhelming. No other book has ever combined such facts and recorded their fulfillment so perfectly.

The Bible tells where and when Jesus was to be born; it speaks of His family, His virgin birth, and tells us why He became man. It records His life by men who knew Him and lived with Him. One of them said, "We proclaim to you what we have seen and heard" (1 John 1:3).

It is interesting to note that the Gospels portray Jesus Christ in four different ways. In Matthew, He is described as the King descended from Israel's royal family. In Mark, He is revealed as the Divine Servant, always busy with His Father's work. In Luke we see Him as the Son of man, closely identified with humanity. In John, His divine nature is emphasized, and He speaks often of eternal life as the sole possession of those who are rightly related to Him.

The Scriptures truly reveal Jesus Christ to us.

2 The Bible Was Given to Reveal God's Plan of Salvation

The Scriptures were given to make us "wise for salvation through faith in Christ Jesus" (2 Timothy 3:15). When the Apostle Paul spoke of "the Holy Scriptures," he was referring to the Old Testament because that's all the people of his day had. He was simply saying, "Timothy, in the Old Testament you will find the plan of salvation which reveals the coming Messiah, Jesus Christ, whom we know and love." That's why we say no one can know Christ as Saviour and Lord apart from the Scriptures.

The New Testament repeatedly describes God's plan of salvation as revealed in Jesus Christ.

3 The Bible Was Given to Help Us Grow Spiritually

When our daughter, Jane, came home from the hospital as an infant, we were delighted, but our responsibility had only begun. We had to make sure she was fed properly in order for her little body to grow. Likewise, when we are born spiritually, we should begin growing. And that growth can only come through our intake of the Word of God. "Like newborn babies, crave pure spiritual milk, so that by it you may grow up in your salvation, now that you have tasted that the Lord is good" (1 Peter 2:2-3).

> In fact, though by this time you ought to be teachers, you need someone to teach you the elementary truths of God's Word all over again. You need milk, not solid food! Anyone who lives on milk, being still an infant, is not acquainted with the teaching about righteousness. But solid food is for the more mature, who by constant use have trained themselves to distinguish good from evil (Hebrews 5:12-14).

Every Christian needs to learn how to hear, read, study, memorize, and meditate regularly on the Scriptures. Whenever a Christian is undernourished spiritually, he is not feeding regularly on the Word of God.

At the end of his third mission, when the Apostle Paul called on the elders of the church at Ephesus, he gave them this challenge: "Now I commit you to God and to the Word of His grace, which can build you up and give you an inheritance among all those who are sanctified" (Acts 20:32).

Old Testament writers also testified of their hunger for the Word of God. Jeremiah said, "Thy words were found and I ate them, and Thy words became for me a joy and the delight of my heart" (Jeremiah 15:16). Job, though severely tested by God, exclaimed, "I have treasured the words of His mouth more than my necessary food" (Job 23:12).

When Jesus was tempted by Satan, who challenged Him to make stones into bread, He responded, "Man does not live on bread alone, but on every word that comes from the mouth of God" (Matthew 4:4).

Christians grow by feeding on the Word of God.

The Bible Was Given to Cleanse Us from Sin

Jesus declared, "You are already clean because of the word I have spoken to you" (John 15:3). Paul said that Christ gave Himself up for His church "to make her holy, cleansing her by the washing with water through the Word" (Ephesians 5:26). The Word of God purifies and washes clean anyone who obeys it. When we take time to read, study, and meditate on the Scriptures, the Holy Spirit in His own gentle way ministers to our hearts and reveals our various sins to us.

When we confess our sins we are simply agreeing with God; what He calls sin, we also call sin. When the Holy Spirit points out sins in our lifes, such as direct dishonesty, lust, or laziness, He convicts our consciences. He then urges us to repent and confess our sins, which results in washing and cleansing us of all sin. We need to pray with David, "Search me, O God, and know my heart; try me and know my anxious thoughts; and see if there be any hurtful way in me, and lead me in the everlasting way" (Psalm 139:23-24).

. Of course, when the Bible shows us our sins, we must act in obedience to have them cleansed. James, the leader of the church at Jerusalem, wrote that, "the man who looks intently into the perfect law that gives freedom, and continues to do this, not forgetting what he has heard, but doing it—he will be blessed in what he does" (James 1:25).

Earlier in this passage, James wrote that a person who does not obey what he reads in Scripture is like a person who looks in a mirror, and then turns away and forgets what he saw. We also can easily forget what we see in God's Word. But God has promised to bless those who look intently into the Scriptures and obey what they see.

One day in Japan, where I had a ministry among U.S. servicemen, I was walking on an errand through an unfamiliar section of town. Soon I realized it was a bad neighborhood. Every form of lustful sin was being flaunted to anyone who wanted it. But God kept me clean through a memorized verse, as the faithful Holy Spirit reminded me, "Do not enter the path of the wicked, and do not proceed in the way of evil men. Avoid it, do not pass by it; turn away from it and pass on" (Proverbs 4:14-15). So I left the area as quickly as possible.

5 The Bible Was Given to Guide and Direct Us

We are constantly faced with decisions. As we mull them over in our minds, weighing the pros and cons, often there seems to be no clear answer. We ask, "Should I do this or that, Lord? What should I do?"

Where do we discover the will of God? In the Word of God! The Apostle John said, "We have this assurance in approaching God, that if we ask anything according to His will, He hears us. And if we know that He hears us—whatever we ask—we know that we have what we asked of Him" (1 John 5:14-15).

God has promised to guide us and direct our lives. He said, "I will instruct you and teach you in the way which you should go; I will counsel you with My eye upon you" (Psalm 32:8).

Solomon expressed confidence in God's guidance: "Trust in the Lord with all your heart, and do not lean on your own understanding. In all your ways acknowledge Him, and He will make your paths straight" (Proverbs 3:5-6).

All of us need divine direction when facing all decisions of life. As the axiom says, "Your life is equal to the sum total of your decisions, both good and bad."

While reading in my devotions in Japan one morning, I discovered this principle: "Every man's way is right in his own eyes, but the Lord weighs the hearts" (Proverbs 21:2). Men seldom admit they are wrong.

I decided to take a survey among the American servicemen. After getting acquainted with several men, I asked each one, "Do you have a girlfriend back home?"

"Yes, I do, and here's her picture." Out would come a picture of his girl.

"What are your plans?" I would ask.

"As soon as I get home, I'm going to marry that girl."

"Have you ever sought counsel about this decision?"

Of the 30 men I surveyed, only two had done so.

"Do you mind if I ask you another question?"

"No, go ahead."

"Is it God's will for your life that you marry this girl?'

I knew what his answer would be. No man in his right mind would answer "No," for it would make him look like a fool.

Here were men ready to make one of life's greatest decisions, yet they had sought no counsel, had not looked for promises in God's Word, had not seriously prayed for God's will, and were about to do something that would change their lives.

God has promised to guide us when we seek His will and submit to the Bible's authority. As we submit, we are then led by the Spirit of God. Let's say, for example, that a young woman has been asked by a young man to marry him. Her suitor is convinced that God has led him, and that she is the one for him. Faced with the decision of responding to this proposal, she turns to God in prayer and asks for His guidance.

She also seeks advice from mature Christians, and continues looking in God's Word for help. Some time after laying this matter before the Lord, during one of her regular devotional times, God clearly speaks to her heart from His Word that this marriage is His will. Now that God's confirmation has cleared away her doubts, she can confidently say, "I know he is God's choice for me."

I've seen this happen in the lives of many people as they trusted God for guidance and the assurance of His will. Today the stability of such marriages remains a testimony to God's faithfulness.

All of us need guidance at some time in our lives. We seek counsel from our pastor, or close friend, then weigh what he advised in the light of the Scriptures. Then we come to a decision. Nothing brings greater peace and confidence than the conviction that we are doing what God wants us to do.

The Bible Was Given to Enable Us to Witness

How can we share the Gospel effectively with someone else unless we know the Scriptures? In 1951, at the beginning of my Navy hitch, I found myself totally inadequate to witness to the men around me. I recognized their poor spiritual condition, but in my ignorance, the only thing I knew to do was to try and win an argument. That method never worked. God does not honor our logic or our arguments—no matter how good they are—but He has promised to honor His Word.

About this time I came in contact with some men who demonstrated a quality of life that attracted me. Their walk with Christ was refreshing and, furthermore, they knew how to witness intelligently and effectively. One of these men started me in Scripture memory, in Bible study, and in vital Christian fellowship. Within three months I had memorized several verses about the Gospel and was able to communicate them to my buddies. Some of them soon began finding the Saviour. I've been witnessing for many years and I never cease to marvel at the power of the Word of God to convert sinners and to enable Christians to witness.

I have also had the privilege of working with the Evangelism Explosion[2] program in our church. This program is designed to train Christians to share the Gospel adequately and effectively. It is the best that I have ever seen, and the results have been encouraging and challenging—my own fruitfulness has increased greatly and I have seen many others become more fruitful.

God has given us His Word essentially for two reasons: first, that we may know Him, experiencing and understanding the Lord and the truth of His Word; second, that we can be ready to give any man answer for the hope that is in us (see 1 Peter 3:15). This is the biblical pattern for all Christians, yet so few are ready to share their faith intelligently.

* * *

How important are the Scriptures? They are absolutely vital to our Christian lives. Paul said the foundation of our lives is Christ (see 1 Corinthians 3:11). And Jesus Christ is the Word of God, the Word which lives and abides forever."

53

NOTES: 1. Addison H. Leitch, *Interpreting Basic Theology* (New York: Hawthorn Books, Inc., 1961), page 46. Reprinted by permission.

2. I highly recommend that every Christian get involved in the Evangelism Explosion program of his church. If your church does not have it, encourage your pastor and leaders to consider starting such a program. Information on Leadership Training Clinics may be obtained by writing Evangelism Explosion III International, Box 23820, Fort Lauderdale, Florida 33307.

3

HOW TO GO ABOUT LEARNING BIBLE TRUTHS

How do we get to know the Bible? How do we reach that stage where we can find any passage easily, or listen to a sermon and understand all that the minister is talking about?

We get to know the Bible by committing ourselves to spending time in it, using all the means available to us of taking in the Word for ourselves. This will allow the Scripture to reveal Jesus Christ to us, to show us His plan of salvation, to give us spiritual food, to purify and cleanse our lives, to guide us, and to enable us to witness to others.

HOW DO WE LEARN BIBLE TRUTHS?

The four means of taking in the Word of God are hearing, reading, studying, and memorizing. In addition, we meditate on what we have heard, read, studied, and memorized. Finally, we apply the truths we have learned to our daily lives. The Hand Illustration pictures the means we have of taking in the Word of God for ourselves (Figure 1).

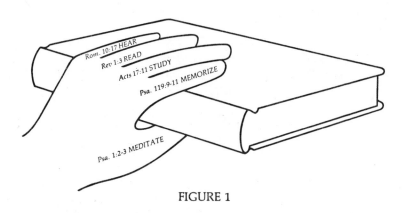

FIGURE 1

Hearing the Word of God

Our first responsibility is to take in the Word of God by *hearing* it. The Bible records that believers in the Early Church "devoted themselves to the apostles' teaching" (Acts 2:42). The apostles of Jesus Christ, the leaders He left behind to build His church, were teaching new believers biblical truths.

The Apostle Paul showed us the importance of hearing when he wrote, "Faith comes from hearing the message, and the message is heard through the Word of Christ" (Romans 10:17). Hearing the Word of God generates faith. It does that because the Bible is reliable and true. When we see what the Bible has to say and recognize the importance of its teaching, we are moved to the point of believing and acting on it.

56

Faith is not a state of mind; it is an action. Faith is a "doing" thing. The Apostle James wrote, "I will show you my faith by what I do" (James 2:18). When some people insist they have faith, others can say, "Well, if that's true, I want to see evidence of your faith." They say this because they know that "faith without deeds is dead" (James 2:26). That's why hearing is important. We hear the Word preached and taught. The Holy Spirit then uses that Word to change our lives, and our faith is built up.

This truth is illustrated in what we call the Parable of the Sower, or the Parable of the Soils (see Mark 4:2-8). In His explanation of the parable, Jesus said:

> The farmer sows the Word. Some people are like seed along the path, where the Word is sown. As soon as they hear it, Satan comes and takes away the Word that was sown in them. Others, like seed sown on rocky places, hear the Word and at once receive it with joy. But since they have no root, they last only a short time. When trouble or persecution comes because of the Word, they quickly fall away. Still others, like seed sown among thorns, hear the Word; but the worries of this life, the deceitfulness of wealth and the desires for other things come in and choke the Word, making it unfruitful. Others, like seed sown on good soil, hear the Word, accept it, and produce a crop—thirty, sixty, or even a hundred times what was sown (Mark 4:14-20).

This parable tells us that the Word of God was being taught or preached. All four groups of listeners heard the same Word, but for three of them other things got in the way—Satan, lack of rooting, worries of life, deceitfulness of riches, desire for things. The fourth group really *listened* to and *applied* the truths they heard, and produced fruit.

The other three listened without application, and bore no fruit.

We must also realize that not everyone is preaching and teaching the Word as it should be preached and taught. Many churches do nothing more than gather the faithful together and preach unnecessary messages to them. Christians do not need to hear the ideas of men. Bible-believing churches are committed to preaching the Word of God.

Most Christians whose only intake of Scripture is hearing it are weak spiritually. It is important not only to hear, but also to meditate on the truths we hear. Then we apply them to our lives.

But hearing is vital and necessary. John wrote, "Blessed is the one who reads the words of this prophecy, and blessed are those who *hear* it and take to heart what is written in it" (Revelation 1:3).

Reading the Word of God

The second way to learn biblical truths is to begin a regular reading program. You can do this in many ways. If you read three chapters in the Old Testament and one in the New Testament each day, you can read the entire Bible through in about 11 months. Or you can read five chapters on Sunday and three on all the other days, from both testaments, and finish in a year. I use a yearly chart dividing the Bible into daily readings (Figure 2).

Most Christians know they should read the Bible regularly, but few do it. Many others read only sporadically. They'll read a chapter today, then two weeks will go by and they'll read a little bit more. Perhaps during a crisis they will turn to the Bible, saying, "Well, maybe the Bible has an answer." But after the crisis passes, they go back to their "Bible-on-the-shelf-for-looks" routine.

Personal Reading Record

Old Testament

Genesis	1	2	3	4	5	6	7	8	9	10	11	12	13	14	15	16	17	18	19	20
	21	22	23	24	25	26	27	28	29	30	31	32	33	34	35	36	37	38	39	40
	41	42	43	44	45	46	47	48	49	50										
Exodus	1	2	3	4	5	6	7	8	9	10	11	12	13	14	15	16	17	18	19	20
	21	22	23	24	25	26	27	28	29	30	31	32	33	34	35	36	37	38	39	40
Leviticus	1	2	3	4	5	6	7	8	9	10	11	12	13	14	15	16	17	18	19	20
	21	22	23	24	25	26	27													
Numbers	1	2	3	4	5	6	7	8	9	10	11	12	13	14	15	16	17	18	19	20
	21	22	23	24	25	26	27	28	29	30	31	32	33	34	35	36				
Deuteronomy	1	2	3	4	5	6	7	8	9	10	11	12	13	14	15	16	17	18	19	20
	21	22	23	24	25	26	27	28	29	30	31	32	33	34						
Joshua	1	2	3	4	5	6	7	8	9	10	11	12	13	14	15	16	17	18	19	20
	21	22	23	24																
Judges	1	2	3	4	5	6	7	8	9	10	11	12	13	14	15	16	17	18	19	20
	21																			
Ruth	1	2	3	4																
1 Samuel	1	2	3	4	5	6	7	8	9	10	11	12	13	14	15	16	17	18	19	20
	21	22	23	24	25	26	27	28	29	30	31									
2 Samuel	1	2	3	4	5	6	7	8	9	10	11	12	13	14	15	16	17	18	19	20
	21	22	23	24																
1 Kings	1	2	3	4	5	6	7	8	9	10	11	12	13	14	15	16	17	18	19	20
	21	22																		
2 Kings	1	2	3	4	5	6	7	8	9	10	11	12	13	14	15	16	17	18	19	20
	21	22	23	24	25															
1 Chronicles	1	2	3	4	5	6	7	8	9	10	11	12	13	14	15	16	17	18	19	20
	21	22	23	24	25	26	27	28	29											
2 Chronicles	1	2	3	4	5	6	7	8	9	10	11	12	13	14	15	16	17	18	19	20
	21	22	23	24	25	26	27	28	29	30	31	32	33	34	35	36				
Ezra	1	2	3	4	5	6	7	8	9	10										
Nehemiah	1	2	3	4	5	6	7	8	9	10	11	12	13							
Esther	1	2	3	4	5	6	7	8	9	10										
Job	1	2	3	4	5	6	7	8	9	10	11	12	13	14	15	16	17	18	18	20
	21	22	23	24	25	26	27	28	29	30	31	32	33	34	35	36	37	38	39	40
	41	42																		
Psalms	1	2	3	4	5	6	7	8	9	10	11	12	13	14	15	16	17	18	19	20
	21	22	23	24	25	26	27	28	29	30	31	32	33	34	35	36	37	38	39	40
	41	42	43	44	45	46	47	48	49	50	51	52	53	54	55	56	57	58	59	60
	61	62	63	64	65	66	67	68	69	70	71	72	73	74	75	76	77	78	79	80
	81	82	83	84	85	86	87	88	89	90	91	92	93	94	95	96	97	98	99	100
	101	102	103	104	105	106	107	108	109	110	111	112	113	114	115	116	117	118	119	120
	121	122	123	124	125	126	127	128	129	130	131	132	133	134	135	136	137	138	139	140
	141	142	143	144	145	146	147	148	149	150										
Proverbs	1	2	3	4	5	6	7	8	9	10	11	12	13	14	15	16	17	18	19	20
	21	22	23	24	25	26	27	28	29	30	31									
Ecclesiastes	1	2	3	4	5	6	7	8	9	10	11	12								
Song of Songs	1	2	3	4	5	6	7	8												
Isaiah	1	2	3	4	5	6	7	8	9	10	11	12	13	14	15	16	17	18	19	20
	21	22	23	24	25	26	27	28	29	30	31	32	33	34	35	36	37	38	39	40
	41	42	43	44	45	46	47	48	49	50	51	52	53	54	55	56	57	58	59	60
	61	62	63	64	65	66														
Jeremiah	1	2	3	4	5	6	7	8	9	10	11	12	13	14	15	16	17	18	19	20
	21	22	23	24	25	26	27	28	29	30	31	32	33	34	35	36	37	38	39	40

FIGURE 2

	41	42	43	44	45	46	47	48	49	50	51	52								
Lamentations	1	2	3	4	5															
Ezekiel	1	2	3	4	5	6	7	8	9	10	11	12	13	14	15	16	17	18	19	20
	21	22	23	24	25	26	27	28	29	30	31	32	33	34	35	36	37	38	39	40
	41	42	43	44	45	46	47	48												
Daniel	1	2	3	4	5	6	7	8	9	10	11	12								
Hosea	1	2	3	4	5	6	7	8	9	10	11	12	13	14						
Joel	1	2	3																	
Amos	1	2	3	4	5	6	7	8	9											
Obadiah	1																			
Jonah	1	2	3	4																
Micah	1	2	3	4	5	6	7													
Nahum	1	2	3																	
Habakkuk	1	2	3																	
Zephaniah	1	2	3																	
Haggaï	1	2																		
Zechariah	1	2	3	4	5	6	7	8	9	10	11	12	13	14						
Malachi	1	2	3	4																

"And now, brethren, I commend you to God, and to the Word of His grace, which is able to build you up, and to give you an inheritance among all them which are sanctified."—Acts 20:32

New Testament

Matthew	1	2	3	4	5	6	7	8	9	10	11	12	13	14	15	16	17	18	19	20
	21	22	23	24	25	26	27	28												
Mark	1	2	3	4	5	6	7	8	9	10	11	12	13	14	15	16				
Luke	1	2	3	4	5	6	7	8	9	10	11	12	13	14	15	16	17	18	19	20
	21	22	23	24																
John	1	2	3	4	5	6	7	8	9	10	11	12	13	14	15	16	17	18	19	20
	21																			
Acts	1	2	3	4	5	6	7	8	9	10	11	12	13	14	15	16	17	18	19	20
	21	22	23	24	25	26	27	28												
Romans	1	2	3	4	5	6	7	8	9	10	11	12	13	14	15	16				
1 Corinthians	1	2	3	4	5	6	7	8	9	10	11	12	13	14	15	16				
2 Corinthians	1	2	3	4	5	6	7	8	9	10	11	12	13							
Galatians	1	2	3	4	5	6														
Ephesians	1	2	3	4	5	6														
Philippians	1	2	3	4																
Colossians	1	2	3	4																
1 Thessalonians	1	2	3	4	5															
2 Thessalonians	1	2	3																	
1 Timothy	1	2	3	4	5	6														
2 Timothy	1	2	3	4																
Titus	1	2	3																	
Philemon	1																			
Hebrews	1	2	3	4	5	6	7	8	9	10	11	12	13							
James	1	2	3	4	5															
1 Peter	1	2	3	4	5															
2 Peter	1	2	3																	
1 John	1	2	3	4	5															
2 John	1																			
3 John	1																			
Jude	1																			
Revelation	1	2	3	4	5	6	7	8	9	10	11	12	13	14	15	16	17	18	19	20
	21	22																		

FIGURE 2

To avoid this problem, commit yourself to reading the Bible regularly and then follow a well-defined plan. Even if you read only a chapter a day, that is worth much more than reading five chapters today and then reading only periodically or only during times of crisis.

The Word of God has much to say about Bible reading. The Apostle John stated, "Blessed is the one who reads the words of this prophecy" (Revelation 1:3). Blessedness—true happiness—comes to the person who reads the Word regularly. The Gospel writers, when recording Jesus' prediction of events to come, wrote, "Let the reader understand" (Matthew 24:15; Mark 13:14). We are not only to read, but also to meditate on and understand what we have read, and apply these truths personally to our lives. What we read must become part of our character.

The Apostle Paul wrote Timothy, "Until I come, devote yourself to the public reading of Scripture" (1 Timothy 4:13). Here we are exhorted not only to private reading but also to public reading of God's Word.

We find this admonition in the Old Testament when God gave instructions to the kings of Israel:

> Now it shall come about when he sits on the throne of his kingdom, he shall write for himself a copy of this law on a scroll in the presence of the Levitical priests.
> And it shall be with him, and he shall read it all the days of his life, that he may learn to fear the Lord his God, by carefully observing all the words of this law and these statutes" (Deuteronomy 17:18-19).

God told the king, the leader of His people, to set a good example by having a private copy of the Law. The king was to read it every day and apply what he read to his life.

Merely reading the Word of God, however, will give us surface knowledge. The person who only reads the Word will understand but a limited amount of biblical truth, and will need other means of intake to grow and achieve spiritual maturity.

Three requirements are necessary for reading the Scripture with understanding: reading expectantly, prayerfully, and meditatively.

1 *We are to read expectantly.* While reading in the Book of Proverbs, I came across the expression "the wise man." So as I read further, I decided to record all the instances where that phrase was used, to see what Solomon was saying about those characterized as "the wise." Consequently, I was able to read with understanding because I was looking for something specific and expecting God to teach me.

If we read the Bible without looking for something or having a plan in mind, we will gain little. But if we are expectant, we will gain understanding. We need to learn to read expectantly.

2 *We are to read prayerfully.* We must also read the Word of God prayerfully, asking God to enable us to see Him and to deepen our relationship with Him. We can pray with the psalmist, "Open Thou mine eyes, that I may behold wondrous things out of Thy law" (Psalm 119:18, KJV). God will answer our prayer, and we will see Jesus. We will see something about His life that is attractive and meaningful to us, for everything in Scripture points to Him.

3 *We are to read meditatively.* To gain understanding, we must meditate on the passage we are reading. We must think through what we read. Our meditation then leads to application. We will discover what God wants in our lives.

With these approaches to reading the Word, you may want to read through the accounts of the lives of biblical characters. God recorded their lives for a specific purpose—to serve as examples of how we should live, and as warnings about what we should not do. The Bible hides nothing, but faithfully depicts a man's life in the manner in which he lived it. When a man's life was rotten and filthy, the Bible portrays it that way. When he was godly, the Bible depicts him as walking with God. Paul stated that "these things happened to them as examples and were written down as warnings for us" (1 Corinthians 10:11). We don't have to do some things to discover they are wrong. The Bible tells us certain things are wrong, and shows us experiences of various people who made those mistakes. From them we can learn valuable lessons.

When I was in the Navy, people would ask me why I didn't do certain things. If I had never experienced them, they wondered, how could I know they were wrong? I knew because the Bible has recorded where a man or woman did that very thing, and was denounced by God for doing it. God spelled out what He thought of that action, and made sure His attitude toward it remained in His Word to give us guidance.

As you read the Bible, look for qualities in people that pleased God, and then copy them in your life. Consider Abraham, for example. He is called the friend of God (see Isaiah 41:8). He walked with God in an intimate relationship. Abraham was both a faithful man and a man of faith. Moses was called the meekest man who ever lived (Numbers 12:3). What is meekness? It is the quality of not defending yourself when you do that which is right. The Hebrew word contains the meaning "God is my defense." A meek person doesn't have to defend his actions or himself; he simply leaves the situation in God's hands. Reading the Word of God enables us to desire these and other qualities, and to begin building them in our lives,

63

Studying the Word of God

To *study* the Word of God is to take a deeper look into the Scriptures. The deeper we dig, the more we are able to grow spiritually. Paul exhorted Timothy, "Do your best to present yourself to God as one approved, a workman who does not need to be ashamed and who correctly handles the Word of truth" (2 Timothy 2:15). The person who studies the Word of God diligently is the workman who is learning to handle it correctly, and who stands approved before God. He is called a workman because it takes work to study. Many Christians do not study the Scriptures because it involves work, discipline, and precious time. Only a small percentage ever study the Word, despite the fact that God blesses those who are willing to make the effort.

Those who do take time to study God's Word are usually involved in a ministry. I once made a survey of those who attended Bible studies at our church. I discovered that those who were studying were also active in evangelism, Sunday School classes, choir, and other activities. They were putting into practice what they were learning in their studies of the Word.

As a Christian, you should be studying the Bible. You should be active in a local Bible study group for your own spiritual growth and ministry. And as you dig into the Word of God, use a pencil or pen and paper to record what you are observing. Learning new truths should be no problem. Many studies are so well-designed that a new Christian or a young believer should have no difficulty with them. Jesus said "These are the Scriptures that testify about Me" (John 5:39). Your study of the Word will deepen your acquaintance with Jesus Christ,

Paul preached the Gospel of Christ in the New Testament city of Berea, and the Scripture relates how "the

Bereans were of more noble character than the Thessalonians, for they received the message with great eagerness and examined the Scriptures every day to see if what Paul said was true" (Acts 17:11). Paul had come to Berea, a city near Thessalonica, and preached to the people in the Jewish synagogue. He preached Jesus as the promised Messiah from the Old Testament. To see whether or not Paul was preaching the truth, they committed themselves to studying the Word of God.

Basics of Bible study. In order for your Bible study to be meaningful and life-changing, you should follow these six basic guidelines:

1. Your study must be consistent. Set aside one to three hours *each week* to study, and ask the Lord to help you be regular in it. Some advanced Bible study groups may want to spend more time.

2. Your study must be systematic. Avoid being haphazard. Don't study one thing one week, shift to something else the next week, and something altogether different the third week. Your study needs a system and an objective.

3. Your study must contain original investigation. The fruit of your study should be what you learned from the Word of God, not what someone else taught you. Ask yourself, *What has the Holy Spirit taught me from His Word? What has He shown me that is mine?* This is not to say that Bible commentaries are not valuable, or should be discarded. Commentaries are the personal investigations and observations of scholars who have studied the Word of God and recorded what the Holy Spirit taught them. But they should be secondary in our own study of Scripture, because we can do the same thing these scholars did.

4. You must record your observations and investigation on paper. In Japan, I would ask men who came

through the servicemen's center two questions. One was, "How's your Bible reading going?" The answers usually showed that their Bible reading was pretty much hit and miss. Then I'd ask, "How's your Bible study going?" I discovered that the vast majority weren't studying the Bible at all, for they had no written evidence of it. They were just reading the Bible sporadically. A big difference exists between reading and studying. You cannot study without reading, but you can read without studying. Study goes beneath the surface.

5. Your study must be applied to your life. When we study the Word, God uses it to minister to us individually. One of the most beautiful aspects of the Bible is that it is always new. A passage we may have read many times will have something fresh and new the next time we study it. That's because our needs have changed, and God uses His Word to meet those needs with new meanings and new answers. This does not mean the Bible's basic doctrines change; they do not. Basic doctrines are always consistent. But the Bible ministers to everyone's life in continually new ways.

Dwight L. Moody once said, "The Scriptures were not given to increase our knowledge, but to change our lives." The Bible tells us how to live effectively in this world. Its truths direct our steps.

6. Your study must be "pass-on-able." You should be able to pass on to others what you have gained from your personal study. If you can't do that, then you made your study too complicated. It must be simple enough to be shared with others. What I have studied over the years, I am sharing with you in this book. A minister does the same thing from the pulpit. All week he studies the Scriptures, and on Sunday morning he transmits the fruits of his study to the congregation. He must be able to com-

municate biblical truths clearly so the congregation can apply those truths to their lives.

Methods of Bible study. There are many methods of Bible study, but we want to look at four basic ones that will help you get started.[1]

1. Question-and-answer Bible studies. Most beginning Bible studies are guided Bible studies. You are given a question and some Bible verses. You look up these Scriptures and, basing your answer on the verses, answer the question in your own words.

2. Chapter analysis Bible studies. Most lifetime Bible study is of the chapter analysis type. You select a book of the Bible and study it chapter by chapter, paragraph by paragraph, using few outside helps. Usually you follow a specific format, such as: (a) What does the passage say? (b) What does it say that I do not understand? (c) What do other passages of Scripture say to help me understand it? (d) How does it apply to my life? This type of study can be done on a whole chapter, a section, a paragraph, or even one verse.

3. Topical Bible studies. Using this method, you study various topics taught throughout the Bible. You choose a topic that interests you and find all the references to it in the Scriptures. After examining each verse or passage carefully, you draw some conclusions. You end your study by applying something from the study topic to your life. Some interesting topics might include faithfulness, the attributes of God, servanthood, faith, salvation, and discipleship.

4. Biographical Bible studies. In this method, you study the lives of men and women in the Bible by examining their character traits. You discover everything you can about that person's life, and then make appropriate application to your life. The lessons you learn can be either

positive or negative. Positive lessons have to do with qualities you want to build in your life, such as faithfulness from Abraham's life. Negative lessons are warnings about those traits you want to avoid in your life, such as the hypocrisy and deceit of Ananias and Sapphira (see Acts 5).

Memorizing the Word of God

The fourth and best way we can learn the Bible is through Scripture memory. The psalmist wrote, "How can a young man keep his way pure? By keeping it according to Thy Word. . . .Thy Word I have treasured in my heart, that I may not sin against Thee" (Psalm 119: 9, 11). Young Christians can keep their ways pure by memorizing the Word of God, treasuring it in their hearts.

Solomon wrote, "My son, keep my words, and treasure my commandments within you. Keep my commandments and live, and my teaching as the apple of your eye. Bind them on your fingers; write them on the tablet of your heart" (Proverbs 7:1-3). Solomon also urged, "Incline your ear and hear the words of the wise, and apply your mind to my knowledge; for it will be pleasant if you keep them within you, that they may be ready on your lips" (Proverbs 22:17-18). Having the Word of God within us—memorized—allows us to be ready to share it verbally with others.

It is wonderful to know the Holy Spirit can use the verses we have put into a compartment of our mind, by drawing them out when we need them. Solomon also said, "When you walk about, they [the memorized Scriptures] will guide you; when you sleep, they will watch over you; and when you awake, they will talk to you" (Proverbs 6:22),

I started memorizing Scripture many years ago. From the beginning, I realized the value of having the Word of

God within my heart so that when I faced a trying situation—a testing or temptation—I had an answer. I began memorizing the Word at the rate of about three verses a week, and I'm still doing it. Why do I memorize Scripture? Because I have convictions about it. I know God wants me to know His word, and He wants me to share it with others, so I discipline myself to add more verses to my biblical vocabulary. I keep adding verses, but I remember that there was a day when I had only one verse memorized. Then came the day I had two, then three, and so on through the years of my Christian life. Each one of us must be personally convinced that it is important to know God's Word and that Scripture memory is one of the most valuable methods of learning it.

The Navigators, an organization I represent, strongly emphasizes Scripture memory.[2] At Coral Ridge Presbyterian Church, where I was a staff member, people stand up in the Sunday evening services and quote a verse they have memorized. To do this, they must take time during the week to learn the verse. This takes discipline, but it is fairly simple to do. You can memorize most verses in five minutes.

Take the next five minutes now to memorize a verse. Start with John 15:7. Begin by reading the verse with its reference five times: "John 15:7, 'If you remain in Me and My words remain in you, ask whatever you wish, and it will be given you,' John 15:7." Then learn each phrase one at a time: "John 15:7, 'If you remain in Me/and My words remain in you,/ask whatever you wish,/and it will be given you,' John 15:7." Now repeat each phrase without looking at it in your Bible. Then put the four phrases together, and you have memorized the verse.

Jesus gave us an example of the importance of the memorized Word of God in His life. During His temptation in the wilderness, He answered the tempter three times with the phrase, "It is written . . ." (Matthew 4:4, 7, 10). He quoted Scripture in His answer to the devil.

Over the years I have found that when I meet a Christian with an attractive relationship with Christ, who demonstrates both doctrinal and practical biblical knowledge, that person memorizes Scripture regularly.

The advantages of knowing God's Word through Scripture memory are many. Key memorized Scriptures serve as "pegs" to knowing Bible chapters and books. If you have memorized John 3:7, which says, "You should not be surprised at My saying, 'You must be born again,'" immediately you know the context deals with Jesus' teaching on the new birth. Memorized Scripture also helps us when we need guidance. We need a word from God when we are faced with decisions, but can't get to a Bible. His Word, stored in our hearts, is readily available for the Holy Spirit to use. Other advantages include help in obtaining the mind of Christ, having personal victory over sin, witnessing, meditation, prayer, counseling, Bible study, public ministry, being an example before others, making us happy, worship, providing a doctrinal foundation, and preparing us for God's use.

Truly, Scripture memory is a thinking Christian's habit!

Meditating on the Word of God

Many centuries ago, God told Joshua after choosing him as the new leader of Israel after Moses' death, "This book of the law shall not depart from your mouth, but you shall meditate on it day and night, so that you may be careful to do according to all that is written in it; for then you will make your way prosperous, and they you will have success" (Joshua 1:8).

Many false ideas about meditation are around today. Eastern religions stress sitting quietly and staring into space or reflecting on an object or sound. Biblical meditation, however, is serious reflection on the Word of God, looking at it from all sides, and tearing it apart in our mind to try to see how it applies to us.

God told Joshua to meditate on His Word day and night. Why did God give him that command? So that he could be "careful *to do.*" We meditate in order to know what a verse's application is, how we should live according to the Scriptures.[3]

How Do We Apply Bible Truths to Our Lives?

We can be absolutely sure of one thing when we are spending time in God's Word: He will speak to us. God will reveal some truths that we need to apply to our daily lives.

The Bible admonishes us to be doers of the Word of God, not hearers only (see James 1:22). The only way this can be made practical is through specific application of what we see in God's Word. Personal applications will change many areas of our life as we ask God to supply the grace to make the changes that are necessary.

Applications are focused on relationships. As you read the Word of God, you will notice God speaking to you about your relationship to Him or your relationships with other people. You may see some truth about how it is important to express your appreciation to Him for His love and sacrifice for you, to praise Him for who He is, to thank Him, and to ask Him to enable you to incorporate these attitudes into your life.

God may speak to you from His Word about submitting a specific area of your life to His control. If He does, you should ask Him to enable you to do so. Narrow it down to a specific thing and ask Him to provide the precise guidelines of *how* you can apply this to your life.

God may also speak to you concerning a specific sin in your life, an attitude problem, or a habit that has been shackling you for many years. He may deal with you concerning your physical body and your care of it. Needless to say, God is concerned with all areas of your life.

God may also speak to you about your relationship with other people. You may find that God is displeased with your unwillingness to go to a friend and right a wrong. The Scripture, through the ministry of the Spirit of God, will reveal this, and you will know specifically what God is talking about. God expects you to do something about it. Most often He will even reveal to you in the Scripture some guidelines of how to go about doing it.

The Scriptures are clear about the need for each of us to obey what God tells us. That's what David did, as he testified, "I considered my ways, and turned my feet to Thy testimonies. I hastened and did not delay to keep Thy commandments" (Psalm 119:59-60).

In applying the Word of God to your life, look for eternal principles that will transform you. One morning I read this passage from the Book of Proverbs: "He who walks with wise men will be wise, but the companion of fools will suffer harm" (Proverbs 13:20).

I remembered Dawson Trotman, founder of The Navigators, explaining the principle of this passage. It was a simple one: If you want to be a man of God or a woman of God, then the best way is to associate yourself closely in friendship with a person who meets that standard. The Bible is full of eternal principles like this which may not be violated by any society of the world. As you ask God to make these principles a part of you, you will find your life conformed more to that of Jesus Christ and to the standards given in Scripture.

A practical way to ensure a personal application is to memorize the verse from which the application has been taken. As you review the verse, you are reminded of the application you took from it. This gives you a further opportunity to pray over it and ask God to make it part of your life.

* * *

In conclusion, let us consider a passage from Paul's writings. The apostle reminds us, "Now finish the work, so that your eager willingness to do it may be matched by your completion of it, according to your means" (2 Corinthians 8:11). In other words, as we feel led by God to do something about our spiritual growth, now is the time to begin working on it. We must move toward the goal of learning Bible truths, asking God to make our listening to His Word, our Bible reading, our Bible study, our Scripture memory, and our meditation on the Word to become a vital intake so our life will be changed to become like Jesus Christ's.

NOTES: 1. The Navigators have produced both question-and-answer and chapter analysis Bible studies. Descriptions of these may be found in *The Navigator Bible Studies Handbook* or in a current NavPress catalog.

2. The Navigators also have a plan for systematically and retentively memorizing Scripture. The key to retention of what you memorize is *review*. *The Topical Memory System* presents 60 verses arranged in five topics. The booklets explain what a topical memory system is and give instructions for both memorizing and review.

3. For further explanation of what the Bible says on this subject, read the NavPress book *Meditation: The Bible Tells You How* by Jim Downing.

4

HOW TO
SPEND
PERSONAL
TIME WITH
GOD

The only way to build a relationship with someone is to spend high quality time with that person. This principle applies to our spiritual lives as well. In order to get to know God and have a fulfilling relationship with Him, we must spend high quality time with Him. This is usually called the devotional or quiet time.

WHAT IS THE DEVOTIONAL TIME?

The devotional time is a special time each day, preferably the first thing in the morning, set aside for fellowship, worship, and communion with God *through the Word and through prayer*. It is a time for study and meditation and reading of the Scriptures. It is a time for God to speak to our hearts and for us to speak back to Him, laying at His feet our praise, our worship, our thanksgiving, our intercession, and our petitions. It is a special time each day when we recognize the vital importance of getting our guidance from Him.

One of the most important aspects of the devotional time is our desire to have it. One of the psalmists expresses that desire beautifully: "As the deer pants for the water brooks, so my soul pants for Thee, O God. My soul thirsts for God, for the living God; when shall I come and appear before God?" (Psalm 42:1-2)

David expressed his desire similarly: "One thing I have asked from the Lord, that I shall seek; that I may dwell in the house of the Lord all the days of my life, to behold the beauty of the Lord, and meditate in His temple" (Psalm 27:4).

David did not ask for ten things, five things, or even two things, but *one thing!* This attitude must be the consuming passion of our lives if we are to get to know God.

Do you have this kind of outlook? Do you have this kind of heart? Are you hungry for fellowship and communion with God? Do you want to wait only on Him? If you do, then He will reveal Himself to you. (See also David's desire as it is expressed in Psalm 63.)

The devotional life is a lifetime of devotion to Jesus Christ. As Paul expressed it, "I want to know Christ and the power of His resurrection and the fellowship of sharing in His sufferings, becoming like Him in His death" (Philippians 3:10).

The Bible and church history are full of examples of men and women who had this vital relationship and communion with God—whose highest desire was to know Him. The greatest example, of course, is the Lord Jesus Christ Himself. Even though He was the Son of God, He knew the importance of fellowship with His Father. At the beginning of His ministry we find Him meeting with God: "Very early in the morning, while it was still dark, Jesus got up, left the house and went off to a solitary place, where He prayed" (Mark 1:35). As His ministry grew and developed, "Jesus often withdrew to lonely places and prayed" (Luke 5:16). Even in very busy times, Jesus continued this practice: "After He had dismissed them [the crowd], He went up into the hills by Himself to pray. When evening came, He was there alone" (Matthew 14:23).

It is wonderful to realize that when we spend time alone with God, reflecting on His Word and on His Person, letting Him speak to us, the Holy Spirit begins changing our lives to become more like Christ's. Before long, others notice that we are changing. It's reflected in our attitudes, our faces, and the way we do things.

Robert Murray McCheyne, a great man of God in 19th-century Scotland, believed in the necessity of the devotional times:

> I ought to pray before seeing anyone. Often when I sleep long or meet with others early, it is eleven or twelve o'clock before I begin secret prayer. This is a wretched system; it is unscriptural. Christ arose before day and went into a solitary place. David says, "Early will I seek Thee; Thou shalt early hear my voice." Family prayer loses much of its power and sweetness, and I can do no good to those who come to seek from me. The conscience feels guilty, the soul unfed, the lamp not trimmed. Then when in secret prayer the soul is often out of tune. I feel it is far better to begin with God, to see His face first, to get my soul near Him before it is near another.[1]

Another worthwhile statement comes from the lips of John Rutherford, a great man of God in England:

I urge upon you communion with Christ, a growing communion. There are curtains to be drawn aside in Christ that we never say and new folding of love in Him. I despair that I shall ever win to the far end of that love, there are so many plys in it. Therefore dig deep and sweat and labor and take pains for Him and set by as much time in the day for Him as you can. He will be won in the labor.[2]

Testimonies of equal fervor could be quoted from the lives of men of God throughout the centuries who spent hours each day in the Scriptures and in prayer.

You may say, "But I don't have that kind of time!" That may be true; most of us do not. But we do have some time to spend with God. No matter how small it might be, it should be high quality time, preferably in the morning before we get started in our busy days. Throughout the years men and women of God have sought Him first. God provided strength and determination to live for Him throughout the day.

We must ask ourselves: *Do others know I have been with Jesus?* Do they know I have been taking the time to get to know Him better? If we have, then it will show clearly in our lives for everyone to see.

A bedraggled, problem-beset woman came to our church offices one day, and I had the privilege of leading her to the Saviour. When she returned about six weeks later, she was so different that I did not recognize her. She had changed so much. She was now radiant, and walking with the Lord. She had been spending time in the Bible, and had been instrumental in her husband's coming to Christ as well. They were now faithfully attending church and were involved in all its activities. Her walk with Christ was obvious.

WHY IS THE DEVOTIONAL TIME NECESSARY?

Why do we need to spend daily time with God? Two major reasons make it important.

We Demonstrate to Christ that We Love Him

The object of our love is usually the object that will consume our time. If we love a person, one of the things that evidences our love is our desire to *be* with that person. If a man is in love with a woman, he will rearrange his schedule as much as possible so he can be with her. Love develops and grows when we associate and communicate with one another. The more time we spend together, the stronger that relationship is going to grow.

My wife and I have made it a priority to have lunch together one day each week. We set aside our busy schedules so that the two of us can spend time with each other and talk over family and personal matters. This lunch is in addition to our daily time together and is vitally important to both our communication and relationship.

In the same way our devotional life is vitally important to our communication and relationship with God. In fact, God seeks the same commitment and time from us. In dealing with the Samaritan woman at Jacob's well, Jesus told her, "A time is coming and has now come when the true worshipers will worship the Father in spirit and truth, for they are the kind of worshipers the Father seeks. God is Spirit, and His worshipers must worship in spirit and in truth" (John 4:23-24). God is more interested in our taking time to be with Him than perhaps we are. God wants our worship; He seeks our communion, He desires our fellowship.

Man was created to have fellowship with God. Adam had fellowship with God in the Garden of Eden. But then

79

sin built up a wall between God and man. The death of Christ on the cross was necessary to break down that wall. Now we can enter confidently into the very presence of God. In fact, we have been invited to do so (see Hebrews 4:16). One of our greatest privileges as Christians is having real communion with God because of Jesus Christ. Strangely, many believers let day after day go by without so much as a few minutes spent in God's presence.

A booklet I highly recommend on this subject is *My Heart Christ's Home* by Robert Boyd Munger.[3] This booklet describes each of our lives as a house divided into many rooms. Each room symbolizes different areas of our lives. God desires access to every one of them, including the closets and the attic. In this booklet, the man of the house walked past the drawing room one day and noticed Jesus Christ sitting by the fireside. He walked in and asked, "Excuse me, how long have You been here?"

The Lord answered, "I have been here every single day."

God is always waiting for and seeking our worship. He wants us to spend time alone with Him in the drawing room of our lives. He wants to communicate with us through the Word and for us to communicate with Him through prayer. It is important that we accept this invitation and satisfy His desire. This is the way we show Jesus Christ that we love Him.

We see this principle illustrated in the life of the psalmist: "I love the Lord, because He hears my voice and my supplications. Because He has inclined His ear to me, therefore I shall call upon Him as long as I live" (Psalm 116:1-2). The psalmist's first expression was, "I love the Lord!"

When was the last time you told Jesus Christ, "I love You"?

We Need the Devotional Time for Our Own Spiritual Well-being

A regular devotional time is of inestimable value to our spiritual lives for three reasons.

It provides spiritual food and strength. When we spend time alone with God each day we are spiritually nourished. All of us receive our necessary spiritual food in that way. It is not enough for us to come to church on Sunday morning, and have communion and fellowship with God there. That only provides spiritual nourishment once a week.

In Western society, most of us have developed the habit of eating three square meals every day. Some of us can get by on two, while others may have two or more snacks in between. The same ought to be true of our spiritual nourishment. As we spend high quality time with God through the open Bible, He speaks with us, shares with us, enriches our lives, and feeds us. So we need our devotional times with God in order to receive the nourishment we need to help us through the day. We should have the same attitude as Job: "I have treasured the words of His mouth more than my necessary food" (Job 23:12).

An incident from the Old Testament illustrates this principle. God provided a special food (called manna) for His people Israel while they were wandering in the wilderness.

In the morning there was a layer of dew around the camp. When the layer of dew evaporated, behold, on the surface of the wilderness there was a fine flake-like thing, fine as hoarfrost on the ground. When the sons of Israel saw it, they said to one another, "What is it?" For they did not know what it was. And Moses said to them, "It is bread which the Lord has given you to eat. This is what the Lord has commanded, Gather of it every man as much as he should eat; you shall take an omer [a unit of measure] apiece according to the number of persons each of you has in his tent." And the sons of Israel did so, and some gathered much and some little. When they measured it with an omer, he who had gathered much had no excess, and he who had gathered little had no lack; every man gathered as much as he should eat (Exodus 16:13-18).

This illustrates the necessary provision God makes for our daily spiritual bread. He provides daily exactly what the day needs. The manna was just what the Hebrews needed for their physical nourishment, and God's Word is just what we need for our spiritual nourishment.

Notice what Paul prayed for the church at Ephesus: "I pray that out of His glorious riches He may strengthen you with power through His Spirit in your inner being" (Ephesians 3:16). God's power supplies the strength we need for each day.

One morning I read this passage from the Book of Proverbs: "Watch the path of your feet, and all your ways will be established" (Proverbs 4:26). I began meditating on this verse, and thought, *Where are my feet going today? What's on my list of activities?* I realized that God doesn't want us to waste our daily lives. He wants every single thing we do to count for Him. He has a plan and a purpose for each of our days. If we are willing to seek Him, He will reveal His will to us and give us the strength to carry it out, and to establish all our ways. So each morning I pray, "Lord, don't allow me to waste my time or get involved in things which will not count for eternity."

Solomon also said, "Commit your works to the Lord, and your plans will be established" (Proverbs 16:3). So I pray, "Lord, this is what I have to do today, and I need Your strength, Your enabling grace, Your power, and everything You can give me to allow me to do what I have to." When I get to my office and I see the counseling appointments I have, the letters I have to write, and the studying I have to do, I am overwhelmed unless I have obtained strength from the Lord. So as I look over my list of activities at the beginning of the day, I pray over it and commit it to God, saying, "Lord, help me today to do the very best job possible." I know the Scripture promises that if I commit my works to the Lord, my plans will be established. This is one of the most beautiful things about our devotional times—we can sit down at the beginning of the day and commit everything to God, and expect Him to give us strength throughout the day.

We have no strength in ourselves to face the pressures of the world; we have no strength to face the onslaughts of the devil; we have no strength to face the temptations of the flesh. But our time with God enables us to overcome.

2 *It provides spiritual victory.* Another reason we need our devotional time with God is for victory over sin. A passage we have already examined states, "How can a young man keep his way pure? By keeping it according to Thy Word. . . . Thy Word have I treasured in my heart, that I may not sin against Thee" (Psalm 119:9, 11). God wants us to have victory through His Word. All of us experience defeat in our Christian lives; we know we fail God. But victory is a matter of choice.

We can choose victory or defeat. The key to victory is to spend time with God daily. When we sin, we simply confess our sins. "If we confess our sins, He is faithful and just and will forgive us our sins and purify us from all unrighteousness" (1 John 1:9). Our time alone with God enables us to have victory during the day.

Something is missing each day if we don't have that time alone with God. The Christian who is not spending time alone with God will have problems, questions, and difficulties. Whenever someone comes to me for counseling and I discover his Christian life is full of problems, I know automatically that his relationship with Jesus Christ is not healthy.

4 It provides joy. The fourth reason for having a devotional time with God is that our lives will become filled with joy. Note how the Prophet Jeremiah felt about being in God's Word. "Thy words were found and I ate them, and Thy words became for me a joy and the delight of my heart; for I have been called by Thy name, O Lord God of hosts" (Jeremiah 15:16). The prophet tells us that when he found God's Word and made it his nourishment, it was a joyful and delightful experience.

WHAT CONSTITUTES THE DEVOTIONAL TIME?

Essentially, two basic things are involved in our times alone with God—reading the Word and prayer. God speaks to us through His Word, and we speak to Him through prayer.

The Word of God

One of Jesus' names in the Bible is "The Word": "In the beginning was the Word, and the Word was with God, and the Word was God. He was with God in the beginning. . . . The Word became flesh and lived for a while among us. We have seen His glory, the glory of the one and only Son, who came from the Father, full of grace and truth" (John 1:1-2, 14). That same Word, Jesus Christ Himself, speaks to us now through the Bible.

84

God has communicated His Word to man throughout history. We read in the Old Testament, "The Lord appeared again at Shiloh, because the Lord revealed Himself to Samuel at Shiloh by the Word of the Lord" (1 Samuel 3:21). In the New Testament, Paul reminded Timothy, "From infancy you have known the holy Scriptures, which are able to make you wise for salvation through faith in Christ Jesus" (2 Timothy 3:15).

The first part of a devotional time with God is to be spent in the Word, allowing Him to speak to us. The Bible becomes a mirror—in it we see both the image of Jesus Christ and our own images in comparison to His. The comparison will show us where we fall short, and where we need to make changes. Many people do not have a devotional life because they do not want to look at themselves in that mirror. They are afraid of what they will see. They are also afraid they will have to make changes they do not want to make. But the Holy Spirit helps us to make the changes God desires.

The psalmist said, "Thy Word is a lamp to my feet, and a light to my path. . . . The unfolding of Thy words gives light; it gives understanding to the simple" (Psalm 119: 105, 130). As we read, meditate, and reflect on God's Word, He reveals His direction, light, and understanding. He may show us His will over a longer period of time, but on a daily basis God provides only the light we need for that day. That's why our daily times with the Lord are so important.

Prayer

Someone has appropriately said that prayer is the voice of our lives. Our spiritual development is revealed by how we pray. In prayer, we bring our burdens and cares to God. We talk with Him about what He has shown us in His Word. We lay requests at His feet; we claim promises that He has made to us in His Word.

Throughout His Word, God makes many promises. We will usually discover a number of them in our reading. We should claim the ones we feel God is giving us, and then pray, "Lord, thank You for giving me this promise; help it to be fulfilled in my life today."

As we have already seen, we are confronted in our Bible reading with sins we must avoid. In prayer we confess our known sins and ask God for strength to avoid those He points out to us.

Prayer was an integral part of the lives of men and women of God throughout the centuries. William Carey, a missionary to India in the late 18th century, wrote:

> Let us often look at [David] Brainerd in the woods of America pouring out his very soul before God for the perishing heathen without whose salvation nothing could make him happy. Prayer—secret, fervent, believing prayer—lies at the root of all personal godliness. A competent knowledge of the language where a missionary lives, a mild and winning temper, a heart given up to God in close religion, these are the attainments which more than all knowledge or all other gifts will fit us to become the instruments of God in the great work of human redemption.[4]

Another great saint of God, Sir Thomas Buckston, said, "You know the value of prayer. It is precious beyond all price. Never, never neglect it."[5] Edward Payson said, "Prayer is the first thing, the second thing, the third thing necessary to a minister. Pray, then, my dear brother, pray, pray, pray."[6] John Wesley, the founder of Methodism, said "Give me one hundred preachers who fear nothing but sin, and desire nothing but God, and care not a straw whether they be clergymen or laymen. Such alone will shake the gates of hell and set up the kingdom of heaven on earth. God does nothing but in answer to prayer."[7]

God does answer prayer. But to receive specific answers to prayer, we must have specific requests. One of the ways in which I organize my requests is to divide a piece of paper into two parts by drawing a line down the middle of a page. On one side I write the word *Requests* and on the other side I write *Answers* (see Figure 3). Then I list all my requests on the left-hand side. For example, I may list a financial need for $100 to pay my dental bills. I don't have the money, but I am going to ask God to provide for that specific need. When God answers my specific prayers and provides that $100 from an unexpected source, I write it down in the *Answers* column.

In 1964, The Navigators invited my wife and me to go to Japan and work among U.S. servicemen. We would have to raise our own financial support for our four years there. In addition, we needed $1,123.20 to ship our belongings to Japan, and for our plane tickets. We had been ministering in Jacksonville, Florida, and were able to raise most of our regular support there, as well as $500 toward shipping and travel costs. I had no clue how God was going to provide the rest. Be we wrote the request down, and prayed.

That summer we arrived at Glen Eyrie, The Navigators headquarters in Colorado Springs, during a couples conference. One evening we ate dinner with a couple at the conference and had a wonderful time getting to know each other and sharing what God had done in our lives. During the conversation I was asked, "How are you doing in raising your support and in getting your cash needs met?" I told them we were still $623.20 short.

Prayer Sheet

Request	God's Answer
To help Rick relax & enjoy his work and to do places	One Answer! his boss told him he needs to slow down.
To help Amelia's foot to straighten out.	

FIGURE 3

The next morning at an early breakfast, this same couple came up to us. The man said, "You know, Francis, after we left you last night we began to pray about your need and felt that the Lord would have us be a part of meeting it." He continued, "My father and another man and I are responsible for giving away $25,000 of an estate of a couple who died recently and who wanted their money to go to evangelical Christian work. I believe you have a legitimate need and I would like to present it to them. I'll call you Friday morning."

That Friday the man called and reported, "The men voted to send you $100."

I replied, "Great! Praise God! That's tremendous. We certainly appreciate that."

Then he said, "Now wait a minute. That's not all. Yesterday I sold 36 head of my cattle. When I returned home from the conference earlier in the week I promised the Lord that any money I made on those cattle that was over $24 per 100 pounds weight I would give to you. While we were at the conference cattle prices fluctuated between $21.50 and $22 per hundredweight. Yesterday the selling price jumped to $25.50, so I am sending you an additional check for $523.20." Do you realize how much money that was? *To the penny* what we needed to go to Japan!

One day I shared this marvelous provision of God with Archie Parrish, Director of Evangelism Explosion III International, and he said, "Francis, I have hundreds of pages just like that. I periodically read them over, and they bolster my faith tremendously. I know God answers prayer, and through these pages I can see the evidences of those answers."

Our daily devotional lives must be a two-way street. When God speaks to us about something from His Word, we need to respond to Him in prayer about it. We might say something like, "Lord, I appreciate that. I really want to obey You and I want You to help me be obedient in this matter."

WHEN SHOULD WE HAVE OUR DEVOTIONAL TIME?

In the Old Testament, David wrote, "In the morning, O Lord, Thou wilt hear my voice; in the morning I will order my prayer to Thee and eagerly watch" (Psalm 5:3). The ideal time for our devotional time is in the morning before our busy day begins.

Family devotions are necessary, but meeting with God in the morning is most effective when you can be alone with Him. Jesus set the example for us, and also taught, "When you pray, go into your room, close the door and pray to your Father, who is unseen. Then your Father, who sees what is done in secret, will reward you" (Matthew 6:6). You do not necessarily have to go to a private room, though that is best. You can shut out the world in the midst of a busy room, on an airplane, or during a lunch break on a busy day in the office. You can pray silently after reading the Word.

This time with God should be regular, even when pressures crowd into our lives. The Prophet Daniel set the pattern for us many centuries ago. When Daniel learned that the king had outlawed prayer to God, we read that "he continued kneeling on his knees three times a day, praying and giving thanks before his God, *as he had been doing previously*" (Daniel 6:10). Prayer was a pattern of life for Daniel, and nothing was going to keep him from it.

In the Muslim religion, adherents pray five times each day, bowing in the direction of Mecca. How much more should we Christians have a commitment to such regularity in meeting with the King of kings and Lord of lords, Jesus Christ our Saviour.

How to Begin Having Devotional Times

Here are some practical guidelines as you begin you devotional times:

1. Determine to set aside some time each day to be alone with God. Young mothers with little children may want to use the time when the children are down for a nap. Those who work nights may take time in the afternoon. Most of us, however, can set aside time in the morning before the day begins. You need to decide what time is best for you, and then stick to your commitment.

Begin with a short period of time and let it grow naturally. One of the best suggestions is to start with as little as seven minutes.[8] It is better to start with a shorter time and be consistent than to start with a longer period and do it only sporadically.

2. Spend the first part of your time reading and the second half praying. In your praying, follow a pattern used by many Christians and remembered easily by using the acrostic ACTS:

A—Adoration → Praise God & His Recognition

C—Confession - of your sins & Ask for his forgiveness

T—Thanksgiving for his help in everything

S—Supplication

A—Adoration comes first. Come into God's presence acknowledging that He is God, and praising Him.

C—Confession is next. When confronted with God, you will realize you have sinned. Ask Him to reveal any sins that are in your life, and then confess them to Him, knowing He will forgive and forget (see 1 John 1:9).

91

T—Thanksgiving is third. Thank God for what He has done for you. Thank Him for your health, for the roof over your head, for the income you have, for the friends God has given you, for your church, for your salvation, and for God's grace to you in all things.

S—Supplication is last. It involves asking. First ask for others (intercession). Pray for the needs of other people as God brings them to mind, and for those on your prayer list. Then pray specifically for yourself and your needs (petition).

3. If you are to carry throughout the day a thought God gave you in your time with Him, you should write it down. To pin down what God is trying to teach you, follow the example of the psalmist, "Open my eyes, that I may behold wonderful things from Thy law" (Psalm 119:18). Write out what wonderful thing He showed you, and how it applies to your life. Figure 4 is an example of a worksheet on which you can record the thoughts God gives you in your devotional time.[9]

* * *

In conclusion, notice this passage of Scripture which summarizes the topic of the devotional life: God told Moses, "So be ready by morning, and come up in the morning to Mount Sinai, and present yourself there to Me on the top of the mountain" (Exodus 34:2). Four things stand out in this passage:

1. Preparation—"so be ready." One of the simplest ways to be ready is to set an alarm clock.

2. Priority—"in the morning." The best time of day is when you are freshest. We must want to give first place to God.

3. Place—"Mount Sinai . . . on the top of the moun-

Quiet Time Worksheet

Translation _____ Year_____

Sunday   Date _____   All I read today _____
Best thing I marked today: *Reference:*_____
Thought: _____
_____
_____
_____

How it impressed me: _____
_____
_____

Monday   Date _____   All I read today _____
Best thing I marked today: *Reference:*_____
Thought: _____
_____
_____
_____

How it impressed me: _____
_____
_____

Tuesday   Date _____   All I read today _____
Best thing I marked today: *Reference:*_____
Thought: _____
_____
_____
_____

How it impressed me: _____
_____
_____

"Happy are those who keep My ways. Hear instruction, be wise and do not refuse it. Happy is the man listening to Me, watching daily at My gates keeping watch at My doorposts." Proverbs 8:32-34 Berkeley

FIGURE 4

Also part of 1 Samuel 2

Wednesday Date _June 29_ All I read today _John Chapt. 6_
Best thing I marked today: *Reference:* _6:35, 6:40, 6:44_
Thought: _"I am the bread of life; he who comes_
to me shall not hunger, and the who believes
in me shall never thirst." That everyone
who sees the Son believes in him should have even
life

How it impressed me: _also saying No one can come_
to me unless the Father draws him. I am
so glad the Lord wants me. It does
make me feel like a new person, and so
loving of him.

Thursday Date _____ All I read today _____
Best thing I marked today: *Reference:*_____
Thought: _____
_____
_____
_____

How it impressed me: _____
_____

Friday Date _____ All I read today _____
Best thing I marked today: *Reference:*_____
Thought: _____
_____
_____
_____

How it impressed me: _____
_____

Saturday Date _____ All I read today _____
Best thing I marked today: *Reference:*_____
Thought: _____
_____
_____
_____

How it impressed me: _____
_____

tain." We need a specific place where we can be alone with God on a regular basis.

4. Person—"present yourself . . . to Me." We meet alone with Him, and give ourselves wholeheartedly to Him.

Now notice what followed after this meeting Moses had with God: "And it came about when Moses was coming down from Mount Sinai . . . that Moses did not know that the skin of his face shone because of his speaking with Him" (Exodus 34:29). His face showed visibly that he had been with God.

When we spend time alone with God each day, we will grow in our Christian life, and others will see that we have been with Him.

NOTES: 1. E.M. Bounds, *Power Through Prayer* (London: Marshall, Morgan & Scott, Ltd., n.d.), page 58.

2. *Power Through Prayer*, page 68.

3. Robert Boyd Munger, *My Heart, Christ's Home* (Downers Grove, Illinois: InterVarsity Press, 1954).

4. *Power Through Prayer*, page 28.

5. *Power Through Prayer*, page 34.

6. *Power Through Prayer*, page 34.

7. *Power Through Prayer*, page 100.

8. Robert D. Foster, *Seven Minutes with God.* (NavPress).

9. These quiet time worksheets are available in two ways: as a *Devotional Diary* (with readings and sheets for one year) or as the *Bible Reading Highlights Record* worksheets (50 sheets in a packet). Both are published by NavPress.

CHAPTER

5

THE
CHURCH
AND
CHRISTIAN
FELLOWSHIP

According to the Bible, a person who becomes a Christian automatically becomes a member of the Church (capital C). Yet in many congregations a person has to attend some type of membership class before he or she is allowed to join that particular church. So we speak of the "church" in two different meanings.

When we speak of the Church in its broad sense, we mean the body of believers in Jesus Christ throughout the whole world and throughout time. Coral Ridge Presbyterian Church, where I attend, is a church—just one manifestation of a local assembly or local congregation in the worldwide Church.

Realizing that the Church, both in its worldwide dimension and in its local manifestation, is God's chosen instrument for reaching the world with the Gospel of Jesus Christ, we need to recognize our relationship to both.

The emergence of the New Testament Church as a distinct entity occurred on the Day of Pentecost, when the

Holy Spirit descended on the gathered believers and empowered them for the task God had given them, namely, world evangelization. On that day, Peter preached a sermon to a large crowd in Jerusalem. A great number of them responded to the call of the Gospel. Luke states, "Those who accepted his message were baptized, and about three thousand were added to their number that day" (Acts 2:41).

This was the beginning of the new form of the people of God. Before Christ, God's people were a national entity—the assembly of Israel—and people became members of it by being born into the Hebrew nation. After Christ's presence here on earth, the Church was formed as a spiritual entity, transcending nationality and race. Entry into its membership is through faith in Jesus Christ.

After the Day of Pentecost, the Church consisted of those who had come to personal faith in Jesus Christ during His ministry in Palestine, plus the 3,000 who had just been converted through Peter's evangelistic sermon. Let us look again at Acts 2:42, where we see that this group of people "devoted themselves to the apostles' teaching and to the fellowship, to the breaking of bread and to prayer." They were under the teaching ministry of the apostles—the leaders of the Church. They gathered regularly to observe the Lord's Supper and to pray.

Everyone was filled with awe, and many wonders and miracles were done by the apostles. All the believers were together and had everything in common. Selling their possessions and goods, they gave to anyone as he had need. Every day they continued to meet together in the temple courts. They broke bread in their homes and ate together with glad and sincere hearts, praising God and enjoying the favor of all the people. And the Lord added to their number daily those who were being saved (Acts 2:43-47).

The church had unity, and gathered regularly in the temple courts and in homes. They worshiped God, had fellowship, and prayed. Here, then, was the beginning of the New Testament Church.

WHAT IS THE CHURCH?

To understand the Church, we need to define it by looking at some specific statements in the Bible.

The Church Is the Body of Jesus Christ.

The Apostle Paul declared, "He [Jesus Christ] is the head of *the body, the church*" (Colossians 1:18). Paul also said, "God placed all things under His feet and appointed Him to be head over everything for *the church, which is His body*, the fullness of Him who fills everything in every way" (Ephesians 1:22-23).

Next, Paul used the metaphor again and described the Church this way:

> His purpose was to create in Himself one new man out of two, thus making peace, and in this one body to reconcile both of them to God through the cross, by which He put to death their hostility . . . Consequently, you are no longer foreigners and aliens, but fellow citizens with God's people and members of God's household, built on the foundation of the apostles and prophets, with Christ Jesus Himself as the chief cornerstone. In Him the whole building is joined together and rises to become a holy temple in the Lord. And in

Him you too are being built together to become a dwelling in which God lives by His Spirit (Ephesians 2:15-16, 19-22).

Here Paul shifted the metaphor from a body to a building, but he teaches the same truth. He returns to the imagery of the body in the third chapter: "Through the Gospel the Gentiles are heirs together with Israel, members together of *one body*, and sharers together in the promise in Christ Jesus" (Ephesians 3:6).

Each believer needs to know his place in the body of Christ. He must recognize that he is related functionally to every other Christian. I need you and your contribution, and you need me. We are interdependent.

Jesus Christ Is the Head of the Church

We see also in these teachings that Jesus Christ is the head of His Church. "He is *the head* of the body, the church; He is the beginning and the firstborn from among the dead, so that in everything He might have the supremacy" (Colossians 1:18). Jesus Christ is Lord over His Church. Paul wrote further, "For the husband is head of the wife as Christ is *the head* of the church, His body, of which He is the Saviour" (Ephesians 5:23).

Our physical bodies are controlled by our heads. Electrical impulses that originate in the brain voluntarily or involuntarily trigger all muscle movements. Our bodies would not move without this center of control. Christ, as the head of the Church, is in absolute control. He is the One who builds His church (see Matthew 16:18). One of the major themes of the Book of Revelation is that Christ is the Almighty One. He examines the churches (Revelation 1—3) and is the King of kings and Lord of lords (Revelation 19:16).

We Become Members of the Church by Personal Faith in Jesus Christ as Saviour and Lord

This is what Paul said about entry into the Church:

> You also were included in Christ when you heard the word of truth, the Gospel of your salvation. In Him, when you believed, you were marked with a seal, the promised Holy Spirit, who is a deposit guaranteeing our inheritance until the redemption of those who are God's possession—to the praise of His glory (Ephesians 1:13-14).

We become members of the Church of Jesus Christ by believing in Him and accepting His gift of eternal life. The Holy Spirit then comes to live in us and becomes the down payment on our eternal redemption. One of the ways we know that we are Christians is through the presence of the Holy Spirit in our hearts. Paul writes further:

> But now in Christ Jesus you who once were far away have been brought near through the blood of Christ. For He Himself is our peace, who has made the two [Jews and Gentiles] one and has destroyed the barrier, the dividing wall of hostility, by abolishing in His flesh the law with its commandments and regulations. His purpose was to create in Himself one new man out of two, thus making peace, and in this one body to reconcile both of them to God through the cross, by which He put to death their hostility (Ephesians 2:13-16).

Through Jesus Christ, racial, national, or cultural hostilities among God's people are dissolved. By personal faith in Him we are all one, and members of His one Church.

101

Creating that unity among us is the Holy Spirit's ministry. "We were all baptized by one Spirit into one body—whether Jews or Greeks, slave or free—and we were all given the one Spirit to drink" (1 Corinthians 12:13).

Paul develops this principle further in his letter to the Galatian church:

> You are all sons of God through faith in Christ Jesus. For all of you who were united with Christ in baptism have been clothed with Christ. There is neither Jew nor Greek, slave nor free, male nor female, for you are all one in Christ Jesus. If you belong to Christ, then you are Abraham's seed, and heirs according to the promise (Galatians 3:26-29).

The Holy Spirit's ministry is to baptize believers into the body of Christ, the Church. When we trust in Christ for salvation and receive His gift of eternal life, the Holy Spirit simultaneously puts us into the body of Christ. He lives inside every true Christian.

The purpose of our becoming members of Christ's Church is to experience changed lives. Paul stated, "Don't you know that all of us who were baptized into Christ Jesus were baptized into His death? We were therefore buried with Him through baptism into death in order that, just as Christ was raised from the dead through the glory of the Father, we too may live a new life" (Romans 6:3-4). When we exercise personal faith in Jesus as Saviour and Lord and become members of His Church, there must be a change in our lives. Our lives must show that we know Christ personally, that the Holy Spirit is living in us, and that we are walking now in newness of life. That's what it means to be a member of the Church of Jesus Christ.

The Visible Church

Two other concepts of the Church are important in this discussion. We can distinguish between what has been called the visible church and the invisible Church. The *visible church* is the body of persons who profess faith in Jesus Christ, who are subordinate to properly appointed or elected officers, and who asociate with those of like belief and practice. They are members of local churches of all denominations, and are found around the world.

Every person who wants to join the church where I attend must be able to share a credible profession of faith. But this is only a verbal profession, since none of us are able to see completely into that person's heart. We cannot know how true that profession might be.

I conduct a large number of New Member Class interviews. I may talk with a person about his faith, share the Gospel of Christ with him, and hear his verbal profession of faith, but still feel that he does not really know the Saviour. That person may even say, "I know Jesus Christ; I believe in Him." And though I may have serious doubts, I cannot prevent that person from joining our church—part of the visible church. If he is willing to stand up before the congregation and answer the questions we ask with the commitment of "I do," I cannot bar him from church membership on the basis of my feelings.

The questions we usually ask are:

1. Do you acknowledge yourself to be a sinner in the sight of God, justly deserving His displeasure, and without hope save in His sovereign mercy?

2. Do you believe in the Lord Jesus Christ as the Son of God and Saviour of sinners, and do you receive and depend on Him alone for salvation as He is offered in the Gospel?

3. Do you now resolve and promise, in humble

103

reliance upon the grace of the Holy Spirit, that you will endeavor to live as becomes the followers of Christ?

4. Do you promise to serve Christ in His Church by supporting and participating in its worship and work to the best of your ability?

5. Do you submit yourself to the government and discipline of the Church, and promise to further its purity and peace?[1]

People usually answer, "I do," to these questions and we have to trust that these replies are sincere.

In the visible church a person bears the responsibility for his profession of faith, and he will have to answer to God. Jesus stated:

> Not everyone who says to Me, "Lord, Lord," will enter the kingdom of heaven, but only he who does the will of My Father who is in heaven. Many will say to Me on that day, "Lord, Lord, did we not prophesy in Your name, and in Your name drive out demons and perform many miracles?" Then I will tell them plainly, "I never knew you. Away from Me, you evildoers!" (Matthew 7:21-23).

Here were members of the visible church who were not truly believers in Christ. By the very fact that Christ will not recognize them, we see that they are not part of the true Church.

Among those who make an insincere profession of faith are people who know that Jesus Christ is the Son of God, that He died on the cross, and that He shed His blood for the sins of men. But they have not personally received Him as their own Saviour and Lord.

Jesus used another metaphor to protray members of the visible church who are not genuine.

The kingdom of heaven is like a man who sowed good seed in his field. But while everyone was sleeping, his enemy came and sowed weeds among the wheat, and went away. When the wheat sprouted and formed heads, then the weeds also appeared.

The owner's servants came to him and said, "Sir, didn't you sow good seed in your field? Where then did the weeds come from?"

"An enemy did this," he replied.

The servants asked him, "Do you want us to go and pull them up?"

"No," he answered, "because while you are pulling the weeds, you may root up the wheat with them. Let both grow together until the harvest. At that time I will tell the harvesters: 'First collect the weeds and tie them in bundles to be burned, then gather the wheat and bring it into my barn'" (Matthew 13:24-30).

Many members of the visible church today whose hearts have never been pierced by the truth of the Gospel are "weeds" in a field of "wheat." The wheat and weeds must be allowed to grow together till the harvest—the Day of Judgment. Then the reality of everyone's profession will be revealed. The same lesson is taught in the parables of the good and bad fish (Matthew 13:47-50) and the sheep and goats (Matthew 25:31-46).

The Invisible Church

The *invisible Church* is the true Church of Jesus Christ and is completely known only to Him. It is composed of all who are truly born again. Jesus describes these true believers as His sheep: "My sheep listen to My voice; I know them, and they follow Me. I give them eternal life, and they shall never perish; no one can snatch them out of

My hand. My Father, who has given them to Me, is greater than all; no one can snatch them out of My Father's hand. I and the Father are one" (John 10:27-30).

The illustration in Figure 5 shows the relationship of the two aspects of the church, visible and invisible.

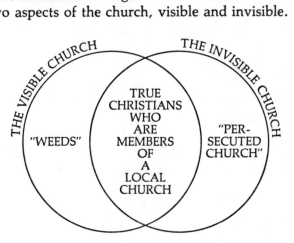

FIGURE 5

One circle represents the visible church, people who are members of local congregations. The other represents the invisible Church, true members of the body of Christ. The overlapping area represents true Christians who are members of a local church. The section on the left that does not overlap, "weeds," represents those members in the local churches who do not really know Christ, while the section on the right, "persecuted church," represents those who are Christians but not members of a local church (for example, believers in countries where organized Christian churches are banned).

One of the most beautiful aspects of the invisible Church is that its members can be assured of their salvation. We can know that we belong to Jesus Christ, and can even know that our Christian friends are real Christians as we see them bear the fruits of following Christ. But we can never make a positive judgment about a person's *not* having salvation if that person says he is saved. Only God can do that.

Belief in Jesus Christ also requires obedience to His commands, and one of these is worshiping with God's people. The writer to the Hebrews expresses it well: "Let us consider how we may spur one another on toward love and good deeds. Let us not give up meeting together, as some are in the habit of doing, but let us encourage one another—and all the more as you see the Day approaching" (Hebrews 10:24-25).

Another command is joining the local church. Consider Christ's Great Commission: "Therefore go and make disciples of all nations, baptizing them in the name of the Father and of the Son and of the Holy Spirit, and teaching them to obey everything I have commanded you" (Matthew 28:19-20). Archie Parrish says that in this passage the procedure to make disciples includes finding, "folding", and feeding the potential disciple. In folding him, "baptize" is used, which is an ordinance of the local church. So whatever baptism means to various Christians, it includes the identification of a believer with a local congregation. Each new Christian must be brought into the fellowship of a local church.

How Do We Relate to the Church?

What is our place in the Church? As believers in Jesus Christ we are members of His body, and we must relate to one another within the body. Paul stated, "The body is a unit, though it is made up of many parts; and though all its parts are many, they form one body. So it is with

107

Christ . . . Now you are the body of Christ, and each one of you is a part of it" (1 Corinthians 12:12, 27). We are each an integral part of the one body of Christ.

Paul also said, "God has chosen to make known among the Gentiles the glorious riches of this mystery, which is Christ in you, the hope of glory" (Colossians 1:27). The church is primarily and fundamentally a body designed to express through each member—every one of us—the life of the indwelling Lord Jesus Christ.

God has placed us in the body where it pleases Him, exactly where we belong. "In fact God has arranged the parts in the body, every one of them, just as He wanted them to be" (1 Corinthians 12:18). Our function, therefore, is vital for the benefit of the whole body. Each one of us depends on other members functioning well in their responsibilities, even as the various parts of our physical bodies must function well together. (For further study in this area, read all of 1 Corinthians 12 and Romans 12.)

No single Christian has all the gifts of the Holy Spirit so that he can make it alone. God made us interdependent. Our gifts complement and supplement the gifts of others. "There are different kinds of spiritual gifts, but the same Spirit . . . Now to each man the manifestation of the Spirit is given for the common good" (1 Corinthians 12:4, 7). When we fail to take our part and carry out our responsibilities, the Church is hindered and limited.

According to the Bible, God the Holy Spirit gives us spiritual gifts for the benefit of the entire body. Perhaps your gift is evangelism; perhaps it is the gift of faith, or the gift of administrations, or the ability to lead and help. Maybe it is the gift of giving or the gift of exhortation—encouraging other people to action. (These gifts are listed for us in Romans 12:5-8, 1 Corinthians 12:4-11, 27-31, and Ephesians 4:11-12). Every Christian has at least one gift;

some have more than one. If you want to discover what your gifts are, get involved serving people in your local church. You will quickly discover your gifts for they are related to ministering to other people. God has given them to you for the benefit of others. These gifts may have nothing to do with what we think are our talents or abilities, or with our secular jobs. These gifts are directly related to our ministry within the local church.

Perhaps I am only a "little finger" of this body; then it's my responsibility to function in the capacity of the little finger. "The eye cannot say to the hand, 'I don't need you!' And the head cannot say to the feet, 'I don't need you'" (1 Corinthians 12:21). We need each other. In each local congregation God will provide the necessary gifts to make it a functioning, effective church.

WHAT DOES THE CHURCH PROVIDE FOR US?

We often ask in life, "What do I get out of this?" In a proper sense we can ask, "What do we get out of the church?" In a local congregation, the entire body contributes to the well-being of its members by providing at least five things.

1. A Place for Worship and Praise of God

The primary function of the local church is to provide a place where believers can collectively worship and praise God. The body as a whole worships together. This is why we have worship services in our churches.

In the Old Testament, Israel gathered regularly to worship God in the tabernacle and in the temple. In the New Testament, Jesus told the Samaritan woman, "A time is coming and has now come when the true worshipers will worship the Father in spirit and truth, for they are the kind of worshipers the Father seeks. God is Spirit and His worshipers must worship in spirit and in truth" (John 4:23-24). The local church must provide the setting where that can be done.

The writer to the Hebrews exclaimed, "Through Jesus, therefore, let us continually offer to God a sacrifice of praise—the fruit of lips that confess His name" (Hebrews 13:15). In gathering for worship, we praise God.

2. A Place for Spiritual Growth

The local church is where Christians are encouraged to grow spiritually. God provided pastors, teachers, and evangelists, to help other believers grow in the faith. Paul says these leaders have been given to the Church "to prepare God's people for works of service, so that the body of Christ may be built up until we all reach unity in the faith and in the knowledge of the Son of God and become mature, attaining the full measure of perfection found in Christ" (Ephesians 4:12-13).

Many churches have Sunday School classes, a strong preaching ministry, Bible study groups, prayer groups, counseling and personal help, a challenging fellowship and training in evangelism. These and other activities aid members in their spiritual growth. Some people do not grow in their Christian lives because they don't avail themselves of these opportunities.

God has given gifted men to churches to help their members grow spiritually. A new Christian cradled in this atmosphere will grow according to God's plan. As we have already seen, this was true in the Early Church. The believers "devoted themselves to the apostles' teaching and to the fellowship, to the breaking of bread and to prayer." They "were together and had everything in common" (Acts 2:42-44), and grew both spiritually and numerically.

We can't help being motivated when we are around people who are going somewhere and know how to get there. Enthusiasm is catching. When our close friends are involved in evangelism, we will want to be involved with them. They are doing something in the kingdom of God and we'll want to do it too. It is one thing to be motivated, but something else to be trained—for example, in evangelism. Realizing this need, churches provide training opportunities for their members.

Of course, pew-sitters are not involved in these training activities. Only hungry believers desiring the Word of God take advantage of the learning situations which churches provide to help Christians grow. And once believers are trained, churches also provide ministry outlets for Christians to use their gifts, for example in such areas as teaching and evangelism.

3 A Place for Family Development

The local church is also an ideal place for strengthening our family units. Many churches today hold family

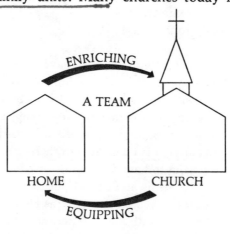

FIGURE 6

conferences to teach their families how to relate better to the church, and how the church can help them in their daily lives. The church equips the Christian home for its life and ministry, while the Christian family enriches the church by its participation (see Figure 6).[2]

My family needs our church. Knowing that I have the responsibility to make sure my family comes under the teaching ministry of the Word of God, I am thankful that my children can attend good Sunday School classes and other training and activity programs at Coral Ridge.

4. A Place for Christian Fellowship

Fellowship is not just Christians getting together. It is a gathering together of believers for the purposes of exalting the Lord Jesus Christ, growing spiritually, and expanding our ministry. Too often Christians get together for coffee and cookies, and call that fellowship. But that's not biblical fellowship. True fellowship must challenge our growth and enable us to do things in harmony with other Christians. We need the mutual friendship and encouragement of other Christians.

The Apostle John wrote:

> We proclaim to you what we have seen and heard, so that you also may have fellowship with us. And our fellowship is with the Father and with His Son, Jesus Christ. We write this to make our joy complete.
>
> This is the message we have heard from Him and declare to you: God is light; in Him there is no darkness at all. If we claim to have fellowship with Him yet walk in the darkness, we lie and do not put the truth into practice. But if we walk in the light, as He is in the light, we have fellowship with one another, and the blood of Jesus, His Son, purifies us from every sin (1 John 1:3-7).

And the Apostle Paul, when he shared his heart with the Roman church, wrote, "I long to see you so that I may impart to you some spiritual gift to make you strong—that is, that you and I may be mutually encouraged by each other's faith" (Romans 1:11-12). This fellowship was a practice of the Early Church (see Acts 2:42).

Some new believers and older Christians do not grow because they do not associate with other believers for the purpose of exalting Christ, serving Him, and growing in faith.

5 A Place for Ministry

Finally, the church is the place for ministry, where committed Christians can have an outreach into the world through evangelism and can disciple new believers. Discipling the believer in the context of the local church was at the heart of the ministry of the Early Church. Likewise, the church today must be the place where that ministry is conducted.

The Early Church in Jerusalem reached out with the Gospel. Luke wrote that "the Lord added to their number daily those who were being saved (Acts 2:47). He tells us about the activities of the apostles: "Day after day, in the temple courts and from house to house, they never stopped teaching and proclaiming the good news that Jesus is the Christ" (Acts 5:42). When a great persecution arose against the church, most of the Christians fled Jerusalem to other regions. This didn't stop their witnessing, however: "Those who had been scattered preached the Word wherever they went" (Acts 8:4).

The local church must be a place from which to launch evangelism, to have a healthy program for those coming to Christ, and to disciple them as they grow into spiritual maturity.

How to Get Involved in the Local Church

A proper church home is one that gives the greatest opportunity for personal growth. The church must preach and teach the Word of God—that's central. Its pastor and leaders must be totally committed to the Lord and to helping other believers grow. Because Christians have the responsibility of getting the message of Jesus Christ to the whole world, the local church must have a strong local evangelism program and a deep commitment to missions—in this country and overseas.

The local church must also provide for the greatest satisfaction of personal and family needs. The church must minister to you at all levels, and you and your family should feel comfortable there. The church must also provide opportunities for you to serve others.

If you find a church that meets these guidelines, you have found a church to join. But once you become a member, don't just sit there. Become active!

Serve Christ through the Church

Get involved in your church's outreach in the community, and serve Jesus Christ by serving the church. Be faithful in your attendance of the worship services, and in your involvement with training opportunities and your church's evangelistic program.

Volunteer to perform needed responsibilities. Many different things in a church should be done by the membership rather than the pastor or paid staff. In our church, we have the "Wonderful Willing Workers." This group of elderly people comes in each week to process the mail, stuff Sunday bulletins, collate printed sermons, prepare our church "Reminder" for mailing, and do a variety of other small but necessary jobs. It is a thrill to see the joy on their faces as they know they are being useful and doing a job that is important. This takes the pressure off the already overloaded staff.

Mothers and teens can serve in the nursery. And the custodial staff can always use some help, as well as those responsible for secretarial work, the church library, and driving the church bus.

Support the Church Financially

The Word of God teaches that we should support the Church and its work with our finances. Scripture also gives us guidelines for this giving. Speaking of money being raised for the relief of their Christian brothers in need in Jerusalem, Paul told the Corinthians, "On the first day of every week, each one of you should set aside a sum of money in keeping with his income, saving it up" (1 Corinthians 16:2).

We are to give joyfully, graciously, and sacrificially to the work of Christ in this world. Paul encouraged the Corinthian church, "Each man should give what he has decided in his heart to give, not reluctantly or under compulsion, for God loves a cheerful giver. And God is able to make all grace abound to you, so that in all things at all times, having all that you need, you will abound in every good work" (2 Corinthians 9:7-8).

The Prophet Malachi recorded how God said:

> Bring the whole tithe into the storehouse, so that there may be food in My house, and test Me now in this, . . . if I will not open for you the windows of heaven, and pour out for you a blessing until there is no more need. Then I will rebuke the devourer for you, so that it may not destroy the fruits of the ground; nor will your vine in the field cast its grapes" (Malachi 3:10-11).

115

I am personally convinced, on the basis of this passage, that God will reprove and rebuke "the devourer" when we obey His words. Who is the devourer? In our day, it is "he" who makes the air conditioner fall apart, the transmission of the car break, the sewer line to get plugged up, and all kinds of other things go wrong, and we must spend money to get them fixed. I believe that in this passage God promises that if we will honor Him with our tithes and offerings, He will keep the devourer of our funds from our door.

We should consider giving to the work of the Lord a great privilege, and do it joyfully. Every local church depends on God to supply funds to meet its needs. God supplies through people who love Him and support His ministry through their giving. Whatever plan your church has, give generously and cheerfully.

* * *

God planned the Church of Jesus Christ for His people here on earth. The local congregation is part of that plan and is God's instrument for reaching the world with the Gospel. It also provides fellowship, encouragement, and a place of worship for Christians. You are an important part of it, and should have a vital part in its ministry, its support, and in praying for the pastor and leaders.

NOTES: 1. From *Application for Membership in the Presbyterian Church in the United States,* used by Coral Ridge Presbyterian Church, Fort Lauderdale, Florida.
2. Reprinted, by permission, from Howard G. Hendricks, *Heaven Help the Home!* (Wheaton, Illinois: Victor Books, 1973), page 20.

6

THE
LORDSHIP
OF JESUS CHRIST
IN A
BELIEVER'S LIFE

One of the most crucial issues in a believer's life is that of the lordship of Jesus Christ. The application of this major doctrine determines whether a Christian will be useful to God and His kingdom. All of our aspirations as Christians and all the blessings and joys of the Christian life are absolutely dependent on our practical submission to Jesus Christ as Lord of all. There is no way whatsoever we can experience the fullness of the Christian life unless we submit to His lordship.

This is an area of great conflict for many Christians. The practice of the lordship of Jesus Christ demands constant submission. It is not like the once-for-all experience of baptism, for example. After we are baptized, it's over, and we don't need to be baptized again. But submission to the lordship of Christ is not once-for-all. We may make an initial commitment to submit to Him when we first discover that He is worthy of our allegiance. But there must also be a day-by-day recommitment to His authority. Jesus

To submit — to commit to the discretion or decision of another or of others.

Christ said, "If anyone would come after Me, he must deny himself and take up his cross *daily* and follow Me" (Luke 9:23).

We are constantly facing new decisions related to the lordship of Christ. It's an everyday battle with the world, the flesh, and the devil. When we compare the temptation and fall of Adam and Eve, the temptations of Jesus and His victory over them, and our own temptations, we find that they are identical in principle. In each temptation we have a choice. We can put Christ first in our lives and resist, or we can put self first and fall. It boils down to the matter of who is first in our lives—self or Jesus Christ.

Whether we are young or old, we face this problem constantly. I have been a Christian for many years, but I'm faced with this issue every day. God through His Holy Spirit will often remind me that a certain area of my life needs to be put under His control.

Is Jesus Christ worthy of being Lord over our lives? Jesus said, "Seek first [God's] kingdom and His righteousness, and all these things will be given to you as well" (Matthew 6:33). The context of this passage deals with our basic physical needs—shelter, clothing, food. Jesus said that if we put Him first in our lives, He will provide those needs. The Bible tells us that He knows what our needs are, and is quite capable of taking care of us.

When we are having struggles, Jesus may be gently laying His finger on an area of our life and asking, "Am I really Lord here or not?"

YES

JESUS CHRIST IS LORD OF ALL

Jesus Christ should be the Lord of each of our lives in a practical way because as God He is already Lord of everything. In Scripture His universal lordship is portrayed vividly, such as in this passage by Paul:

> He is the image of the invisible God, the firstborn over all creation. For by Him all things were created: things in heaven and on earth, visible and invisible, whether thrones or powers or rulers or authorities; all things were created by Him and for Him. He is before all things, and in Him all things hold together. And He is the head of the body, the church; He is the beginning and the firstborn from among the dead, so that in everything He might have the supremacy (Colossians 1:15-18).

Jesus Christ occupies the place of preeminence; He is at the very top of all things; He is Lord God Almighty. Once we see what He is like, we can submit to Him and recognize practically that He is Lord.

Jesus Christ Is the Creator and Sustainer of All Things

The Colossians passage above and others tell us that Jesus Christ created all things. His power is absolutely without limit and without end.

If you were to go into the Everglades here in Florida, away from the lights of the cities, and look up at the skies on a clear night, you could probably see thousands of stars with your naked eye. If you used an ordinary telescope or a pair of binoculars, you could perhaps see millions of stars. And if you were to go to Mount Palomar in Southern California and look at the sky through the 200-inch telescope at the observatory, you could see countless more.

In fact, scientists don't even try to count the number of stars anymore. And the universe is so large that they talk in terms of light years to measure distances. (A light year is the distance light travels in one year at the speed of 186,000 miles per second.) A single light year is trillions of miles. These distances boggle our minds, for there is no end of space in sight. The Lord Jesus Christ created all this and more.

If you were able to fire a bullet in such a way that it traveled around the world at the speed of light, we are told that before you had completely released the trigger the bullet would have gone through your body seven times. And it is estimated that if we travel at the speed of light from the earth to the edge of our galaxy—the Milky Way—it would take 100,000 years. And there are uncountable numbers of other galaxies beyond. There are an estimated 30,000 galaxies larger than our own located in the area of sky in the pan of the Big Dipper constellation in our northern sky. Jesus Christ created all of them and more, according to the Bible.

When we consider the microscopic world, we discover an infinite number of forms of life that exist in it. Jesus Christ also created all these.

Not only did Jesus Christ create these things, but He is in control of it all and keeps everything going. By Him all things are held together. By His powerful word all creation is sustained. If He let go, the universe would instantly become chaotic. (See Hebrews 1:2-3.)

All but one of the Lord's creations—man—are in submission to Him. All things follow the laws which have been designed to govern them except man, who has not followed the law of God found in his conscience or written in God's Word. Men are in rebellion against God, and they go their own way. They do not submit to the Creator. The evidence for this is all around us, and is described by Paul in Romans 1:18—3:20.

Jesus Christ Is the Redeemer of Men

God in His love, mercy, and grace, redeemed us from our sins by sending His Son, Jesus Christ, to earth to take the punishment of our sins on Himself. By virtue of Christ's death on our behalf, He has the right to be Lord of our lives.

A person who does not know Jesus Christ resists His rule over his life. But a greater problem is that often the Christian also resists the lordship of Christ over his life. All the problems in a Christian's life can be traced to two major reasons—sin and a lack of submission to Jesus Christ. Sin is a problem because it is always with us through the temptations of the world, the flesh, and the devil.

As for the second reason, all of us resist His rule to some degree. We don't always want Him to rule our lives. This resistance is the reason many Christians do not sense the presence of God in their lives, and wonder why their walk with Christ is so cold, and why they have so many problems. It is all due to their lack of surrender and submission to Jesus Christ as Lord. He is stifled and held back. He wants to give us the fullest life we could ever experience, yet in the hardness of our hearts we refuse to submit to Him.

When Jesus was on earth, He told people that He had come so that men "may have life, and have it to the full" (John 10:10). The degree of abundance we experience in our lives depends on how much we are willing to surrender and submit to Jesus as Lord of our lives.

By nature I want to be first in my life. This is something I have inherited from my forefather Adam. Even as a Christian, I struggle with it. Jesus Himself faced this temptation, but prevailed over it: "I have come down from heaven not to do My will but to do the will of Him who sent Me" (John 6:38). Jesus was the only person who ever lived who absolutely obeyed and submitted to His heavenly Father.

On another occasion Jesus said, "My food is to do the will of Him who sent Me and to finish His work" John 4:34). In the midst of a busy day, after He had ministered to the Samaritan woman at the well and led her to a knowledge of Himself, the disciples had approached Him with food they bought in the nearby town. Jesus said, in effect, "I don't have time to eat; My responsibility is to do the will of God." He was in total submission to the Father. Yet He encountered conflict in this area, for we find Him praying in agony in the Garden of Gethsemane, "My Father, if it is possible, may this cup [of suffering] be taken from Me. Yet not as I will, but as You will" (Matthew 26:39). He struggled, but He emerged victorious.

The Bible tells us that Jesus "has been tempted in every way, just as we are—yet was without sin" (Hebrews 4:15). Jesus understands the conflicts we have in submitting to Him.

We must realize, however, that we are no longer our own. By virtue of Christ's death on the cross and His buying us out of sin, we now belong to Him. Paul said, "Do you not know that your body is a temple of the Holy Spirit, who is in you, whom you have received from God? You are not your own; you were bought at a price. Therefore honor God with your body" (1 Corinthians 6:19-20).

JESUS CHRIST IS OUR LORD

For our submission to Christ to be personal and practical we must follow some requirements related to our acknowledgment of His lordship in our daily lives.

Surrender of All We Possess

The first requirement is to surrender all we possess to Jesus Christ, in spite of our tendency to want to hold on tightly to the things we own. Jesus said, "Any of you who does not give up everything he has cannot be My disciple" (Luke 14:33).

The story is told of a Christian businessman who owned several farms in Nebraska. He lived in a city and had hired another man to manage them. One day the businessman received a telegram from his manager. It began with the words "I QUIT," and proceeded to tell of an impending catastrophe for which the manager did not want to be responsible. A horde of grasshoppers, eating everything in their path, was heading straight for his farms.

When the businessman had been given the bad news, he was asked, "Well, what are you going to do?"

The man answered, "If God wants to feed His grasshoppers on His grain, I can't do anything about it!" This man's possession had been committed to the Lord.

Undoubtedly such a commitment is hard to make because it is contrary to human nature. But it does separate the disciples from the also-rans, as evidenced by the response Jesus received when He demanded commitment from His followers: "From this time many of His disciples turned back and no longer followed Him" (John 6:66).

What about your home? Your car? Perhaps your boat? Your furniture? Your bank account? Your stocks and bonds? How do you hold them? Jesus Christ must be Lord of all our possessions. They are really His and are only entrusted to you.

During my four years in Japan working with American servicemen, I was amazed at how the military personnel grasped for more possessions. Even some Christians seemed to be concerned primarily with the acquisition of material things. Here in Fort Lauderdale, many people own very expensive boats and yachts that ply the Intracoastal Canal and the other waters around us. Many of their owners always seem to want something bigger, better, and faster. Paul said of people like this, "Their mind is on earthly things" (Philippians 3:19).

God "richly provides us with everything for our enjoyment" (1 Timothy 6:17), but we should not grasp these things greedily to ourselves. We must acknowledge that they really belong to God. We must make sure that He is the Lord of all our possessions.

Giving Control of All Our Plans to God

Another requirement is that we put all our plans in God's hands. Too often we make our plans and then ask God to "rubber stamp" what we laid out without consulting Him.

One day I received a phone call from a man I knew who was seeking counsel about a major decision he was facing. The Bible teaches us that "in abundance of counselors there is victory" (Proverbs 11:14). But I hadn't talked with him long before I realized he had already made his decision and simply wanted me to approve it. His call was only for the purpose of soothing his conscience. It is often that way between us and God: "Lord, I've made these plans, so please put Your OK on them!" That is not living under the lordship of Christ.

His Way Is Best

God places His finger on areas of our lives that are not surrendered to Him, because He wants to give us something far better. We see this principle illustrated in the New Testament story of the rich young ruler. He came to

Jesus seeking to inherit eternal life. "Jesus looked at him and loved him. 'One thing you lack,' He said. 'Go, sell everything you have and give to the poor, and you will have treasure in heaven. Then come, follow Me'" (Mark 10:21). Tragically, the young man couldn't do it. His love for his possessions kept him from the treasures Jesus offered.

God doesn't want us necessarily to sell all our possessions. He has given riches to some so that the money can be used for Him and His glory. However, He does want us to hold all our possessions with an open hand.

In the Orient and in Africa, people catch monkeys by putting nuts or fruit in a narrow-neck jar chained to a tree. When the monkey grabs the bait, it cannot pull its enlarged fist back through the narrow neck of the jar. But the monkey refuses to let go, and is trapped because of its greed. The same principle is often true of us. We hold on greedily to our possessions, and we suffer because we will not let them go.

One responsibility of the Holy Spirit is to make us aware of such areas of our lives that should be surrendered to Jesus Christ. Total surrender is certainly a struggle, but we must do it even though we don't feel like it. "I just can't do it!" must not be in the vocabulary of a Christian. In Christ, we can do anything. We will never become what God intends us to be without complete surrender to Him of all that we are and have. Jesus said, "No one can serve two masters. Either he will hate the one and love the other, or he will be devoted to the one and despise the other. You cannot serve both God and Money" (Matthew 6:24). In my Bible, I have written the word LORDSHIP next to this verse. The issue is simply this: Am I content with what I have or am I grasping for more?

I am a model railroader, and have enjoyed this hobby

for many years. I love to work with model trains and often make my own engines from "scratch." Using sheets of brass, pieces of metal, and pieces of wood, I build my own brass engines, some of which have won top honors in Florida and nationally. I often see beautiful equipment at conventions and in hobby shops, and I think, *Boy, I would really like to have one of those. It's so beautiful!* Then the Holy Spirit reminds me, "Francis, watch that grasping after!" Since my hobby is surrendered to the lordship of Christ, I only spend time and money on it that He allows me to spend.

The following Pie Illustration (Figure 7) is the best I've seen for communicating the principle of the lordship of Christ. Each segment of the "pie" represents a major area of our lives where there is often a struggle over who will be lord—me or Jesus Christ. Study the diagram carefully and evaluate your life by it. Notice that one segment is left blank—it can represent a personal area of conflict not pictured.

The issue boils down to the same one that confronted the Israelites in the last days of Joshua. "Choose for yourselves today whom you will serve," he challenged them. "But as for me and my house, we will serve the Lord" (Joshua 24:15). We, too, have that choice to make—daily. Whom will we serve? Ourselves or Christ? God or Money?

We cannot remain on the fence. We cannot fluctuate between wholeheartedly serving Christ and His Church, and living in the world as well. Our allegiance has to be to the one or to the other.

If we have unsurrendered areas in our lives, we are selling ourselves short. God does not want our lives to be mundane and meaningless. But in order for them to have meaning, we have to live His way.

126

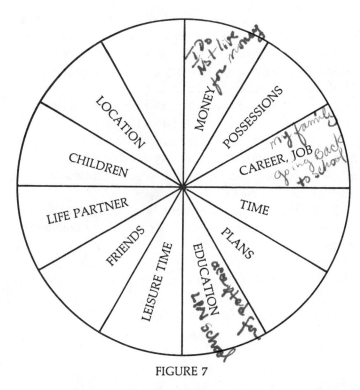

FIGURE 7

We find an example of this in the early ministry of Jesus. Andrew, a fisherman, came to Jesus and began to follow Him. He then went to his brother, Simon, and told him about finding the Messiah. So Simon came to Jesus, who looked at him and said, "You are Simon, the son of John. You will be called Cephas" (John 1:42). Cephas, translated Peter, means "rock." Jesus knew what Simon Peter could become—a rock of faith—by the grace of God. For three years Peter was in training. During that time he made many mistakes, but at the end of that time—after the Resurrection—he became a dynamic leader in the Early Church (read the Book of Acts).

127

It is marvelous to see God reaching down, picking men and women from the gutters of life and remaking them into the image of Jesus Christ. Every week people who live in misery come into my office. I share the Gospel with them, they reach out to Jesus Christ and receive Him by faith, He forgives their sins, and God makes them into new men and women in Christ. This is God's grace in operation. This is Christianity in its true form. And this is what Jesus did with Peter. Today God looks at all of us and sees what we can become if we will submit to Jesus Christ as Lord of our lives.

Rod Sargent, vice-president of development for The Navigators, shared this poem in a message he delivered on the lordship of Christ:

> One by one He took them from me,
> All the things I *valued* most,
> Until I was empty-handed;
> Every glittering toy was lost.
>
> And I walked earth's highway grieving
> In my rags and poverty,
> Til I heard a voice inviting,
> "Lift those empty hands to Me."
>
> And I held my hands toward heaven
> And He filled them with a store
> Of His own abundant riches,
> Till they could contain no more.
>
> And at last I contemplated
> With my stupid mind and soul
> That God could not pour riches
> Into hands already full.

Jesus Is Lord Whether We Want Him to Be or Not

In his excellent book *Disciples Are Made—Not Born,* Walt Henrichsen does a masterful job of speaking to this issue:

> Have you ever considered how little of your life you control? Did you decide when you would be born? Or who your parents would be? Or in what country you would be born? Did you decide the color of your skin? Your eyes? Your hair? Did you decide your intelligence or your gifts and talents? How about your height—did you determine that? Or your appearance, whether you would be good looking or rather plain? The answer to all these questions is no. In every one of these areas and in many more, you have no say in the matter. Your vote counts for absolutely nothing!
>
> Then at what point do you exercise control? The Bible suggests that you control a small but important part of your life, namely your will. Lordship has to do with your will. It involves surrendering it to Jesus Christ. It means that Jesus is Lord of all of you, not just part of you. In making this decision of the will, remember that He has control over most things that concern you, whether you like it or not.

WHY WE DO NOT WANT TO ACKNOWLEDGE CHRIST AS LORD

Though every person has his own reasons not to acknowledge Jesus as Lord, some reasons come up with remarkable frequency.

1. *He may ask us to do something that we do not want to do.*

Of course, He will. If this were not so, there would

be no issue involved. When you make Jesus Christ Lord of your life, you can count on Him asking you to do things you would rather not do.

Abraham did not want to offer up Isaac as a sacrifice. Moses did not want to go before Pharaoh. Joseph did not want to spend all those years in prison. Jesus Christ did not want to go to the cross.

Nobody likes the cross. Nobody likes to die. Nobody likes to deny himself. But this is what lordship is all about. A disciple is a *disciplined* one. He is one who says no to what he wants in deference to what his Lord wants. The disciple does not pamper himself by satisfying his wants and desires in a self-gratifying fashion.

When Jesus Christ is Lord of your life, every area is under His jurisdiction—your thoughts, your actions, your plans, your vocation, your leisure time, and your life goal. All of these are under His lordship.

2. *We think we know what is best for us.*

Nothing could be farther from the truth. A child left alone would kill himself. He might eat the wrong things, or run out in the street, or grab hold of a sharp knife, or play with something equally dangerous. The parent must keep constant watch over his child. That is, the parent must be lord of the child's life. In fact, the law requires that this be so; and when the parent refuses to exercise such lordship, the courts hold him accountable.

When we reach physical maturity, however, we think that things suddenly change. This is where we make our mistake. A child left to himself will probably hurt himself. As mature adults, left to ourselves, we *do* hurt ourselves. Statistics reveal that more people die each year in automobile accidents than by cancer and heart disease combined.

A group of scientists have warned that the United

States has enough atomic warheads to destroy every human being on the face of the earth—the equivalent of one railroad boxcar load of dynamite for every man, woman, and child in the world. And this is to say nothing about the atomic warheads that other nations of the world have.

Have you ever thought about the fact that we hire policemen to watch over us to make sure that we don't do anything wrong? Yet, we have the audacity to say that we know what is best for our lives.

3. *We are not sure that God has our best interest at heart.*

If God wanted to make it hard on us, can you imagine what He could do? If He wanted to make us miserable and plague us with difficulties, He could make life absolutely intolerable.

One might argue that God does not want to get involved in our lives, but it is ridiculous to say that He wants to hurt us.

However, you cannot argue that Jesus Christ does not want to get involved in your life. The very issue of lordship revolves around the fact that He *does* want to get involved in your life. Listen to what He says through the prophet Jeremiah. "'For I know the plans I have for you,' says the Lord. 'They are plans for good and not for evil, to give you a future and a hope'" (Jeremiah 29:11, LB).[1]

In conclusion, the issue of the lordship of Christ is the most critical of any Christian's life. We are all aware of those around us who are reaping in their lives the byproducts of their lack of obedience. Christ has our very best interest at heart. We must give Him our life—our future, our present, our past. We must live only for Him daily. Only then do we experience the full life He has promised.

NOTE: 1. Walter A. Henrichsen, *Disciples are Made—Not Born* (Wheaton, Illinois: Victor Books, 1974), pages 20-23.

CHAPTER

7

THE
IMPORTANCE
OF BEING
CHRIST'S
DISCIPLE

Jesus Christ gave His last command to His followers just prior to His ascension: "All authority in heaven and on earth has been given to Me. Therefore go and make disciples of all nations, baptizing them in the name of the Father and of the Son and of the Holy Spirit, and teaching them to obey everything I have commanded you. And surely I will be with you always, to the very end of the age" (Matthew 28:18-20). This command, often called the Great Commission, applies to Christians in all generations.

What did Jesus mean by the statement, "Go and make disciples"? What is a disciple? How will we know when we have made one? Are we equipped to make disciples?

THE CONCEPT OF DISCIPLESHIP

The simplest definition of a disciple is that he or she is a learner, a follower. A dedicated communist might be called a disciple of Karl Marx. There are disciples of Muhammad, of Mormonism, and of many other people and causes. In the Bible, John the Baptist had followers who were known as his disciples.

When Jesus began His public ministry, He attracted followers who became known as His disciples. They were asked to give total allegiance to the Lord. He declared that His disciples were to follow Him wholeheartedly. *Christian discipleship is an all-out commitment to Jesus Christ as Lord of our lives.* William MacDonald has written:

> True Christianity is an all-out commitment to the Lord Jesus Christ.
>
> The Saviour is not looking for men and women who will give their spare evenings to Him or their weekends or their years of retirement. Rather He seeks those who will give Him first place in their lives.[1]

H. A. Evan Hopkins wrote of Jesus Christ:

> He looks today as He ever looks, not for crowds drifting aimlessly in His track, but for the individual man or woman whose undying allegiance will spring from their having recognized that He wants those who are prepared to follow Him through the path of self-renunciation which He trod before them.[2]

Nothing less than an unconditional surrender could be fitting to the sacrifice of Calvary. Isaac Watts wrote:

> When I survey the wondrous cross
> On which the Prince of Glory died,
> My richest gain I count but loss,
> And pour contempt on all my pride.

Were the whole realm of nature mine,
That were a present far too small;
Love so amazing, so divine,
Demands my soul, my life, my all.

The Lord Jesus made stringent demands on those who would follow Him—demands all but overlooked in these days of luxurious and easy living. Too often we look on Christianity as an escape from hell and a guaranteed ticket to heaven. Beyond that we feel we have every right, along with the rest of the world, to enjoy the best this life has to offer. We know there are some strong statements in the Bible, but we have difficulty reconciling them with our preconceived ideas of what Christianity ought to be.

We accept the fact that soldiers give their lives for their country for patriotic reasons. We do not think it strange that communists give their lives for political reasons. Yet the concept that blood, sweat, and tears should characterize the life of a genuine follower of Christ somehow seems remote. Yet the words of the Master are clear: "If anyone would come after Me, he must deny himself and take up his cross daily and follow Me" (Luke 9:23). There is no room for misunderstanding in these words; the terms *anyone, must deny himself, take up his cross daily,* and *follow Me* must be taken at face value.

A friend of mine has said, "Discipleship is our opportunity to tap the infinite resources of God. It is our chance to give our lives to significance, rather than mediocrity."[3] Jesus Christ lays the claims of Christian discipleship before every one of us who says he belongs to Him. He confronts us with a choice: the path of discipleship or the path of mediocrity (see Figure 8).

I have seen these choices presented, taken, and their results lived out. I have seen young men and women con-

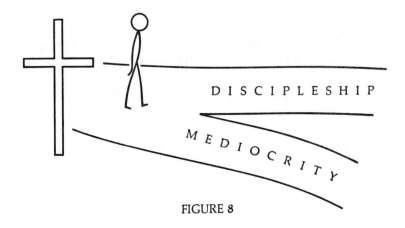

FIGURE 8

fronted by these choices. Some would choose the path of discipleship, and eventually become leaders for Jesus Christ. Others chose the other path, and their lives became mediocre.

We can chart the choice this way (Figure 9). The cross represents our spiritual birthday, the day we met and received Jesus Christ as Saviour and Lord. God's plan for us (the straight horizontal line) is that we become true disciples. But it is amazing to note how many have opted for mediocrity later in their Christian lives. Our churches are full of multitudes who have chosen that way.

God wants all Christians to be His disciples, but the choice is up to us. It usually takes about one year for a person to develop into a Christian disciple, and another year or two for him to become a disciplemaker, a person who in turn produces other disciples. This is God's plan: A new believer becomes a disciple; he is trained, and eventually is equipped by God to produce other disciples. This is the plan Jesus meant in the Great Commission: "Go and make disciples!"

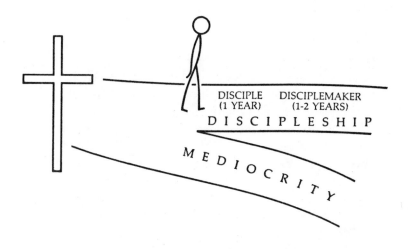

FIGURE 9

THE TERMS OF DISCIPLESHIP

Becoming a disciple doesn't happen by osmosis. It comes through a commitment to the terms of discipleship. Each one of us must evaluate our own lives in light of Jesus' requirements.[4]

A Supreme Love for Jesus Christ

A disciple of Jesus Christ must have a supreme love for the Saviour. Jesus said, "If anyone comes to Me and does not hate his father and mother, his wife and children, his brothers and sisters—yes, even his own life—he cannot be My disciple" (Luke 14:26).

People often have trouble with the word *hate* in this passage. Yet Jesus uses it to emphasize the critical truth that we cannot love anyone more than we love Him. We

137

ESSENTIALS OF NEW LIFE

might read Jesus' statement this way: "If anyone comes to Me and *loves* his father and mother, his wife and children, his brothers and sisters—yes, even his own life—*more than Me,* he cannot be My disciple." Jesus Christ tolerates no rival in our lives if we are to be His disciples. He is either supreme in the throne room of our lives or He is not. He is either the preeminent One or He is not.

The major conflict for many of us is not so much with parents or families, but with our own lives. Self-love placed above love for Christ is the reason many choose the road to mediocrity.

I realized this teaching in my own life early in my marriage. My wife, Norma, and I had been married less than a week when this statement (Luke 14:26) confronted me one day as I was spending some time alone with God. I became aware that though I loved my wife very much (and I love her even more today), she could never take the place of Jesus Christ in my life. I realized that all human relationships must be on a different level than my relationship with Jesus Christ. I must love Him supremely.

A Denial of Self

Jesus calls His disciples to a denial of self. He said, "If anyone would come after Me, he must deny himself and take up his cross and follow Me" (Matthew 16:24). Denial of self is the total abdication of self from the throne of our lives, and is not the same as self-denial, which can be simply foregoing certain pleasures, luxuries, or actions.

Henry Martyn, a great man of God, said, "Lord, let me have no will of my own, or consider my true happiness as depending in the smallest degree on anything that can befall me, but as consisting altogether in conformity to Thy will."[5] When self abdicates the throne, Jesus can come in and have free reign.

138

A Deliberate Choosing of the Cross

The third term of Christian discipleship is our deliberate choosing of the cross. Jesus said, "If anyone would come after Me, he must deny himself and take up his cross daily and follow Me" (Luke 9:23). The cross here is identification with Christ and His cross. It does not refer, as some Christians have said, to particular infirmities or burdens we may sometimes have to bear. Nonbelievers also have to bear those same infirmities and burdens. Jesus means the cross of identification with Him.

The world hated Jesus Christ; the world will hate us. The world was an enemy to Christ; the world is an enemy to us. The world could never in itself be reconciled to Jesus Christ. The world can never be reconciled to the true Christian Church. When we take up our cross we are identifying with Him. We are saying that in Christ we are ready to take whatever the world throws against us.

We see this identification in the life of Paul. Because of it, the world of his day heaped abuse on him:

> I have worked much harder, been in prison more frequently, been flogged more severely, and been exposed to death again and again. Five times I received from the Jews the forty lashes minus one. Three times I was beaten with rods, once I was stoned, three times I was shipwrecked, I spent a night and a day in the open sea, I have been constantly on the move. I have been in danger from rivers, in danger from bandits, in danger from my own countrymen, in danger from Gentiles; in danger in the city, in danger in the country, in danger at sea; and in danger from false brothers. I have labored and toiled and have often gone without sleep; I have known hunger and thirst and have often gone without food; I have been cold and naked (2 Corinthians 11:23-27).

139

Can we expect anything less than what Paul endured? We may respond, "But we live in the United States in the 20th century." Most of us in the Western world do have many conveniences and liberties. But in our hearts there should be no reason to expect less than Paul experienced if we are to follow Jesus Christ. The real conflict for us is whether we will follow Christ's way or our own.

A book I recommend highly is *Foxe's Book of Martyrs*.[6] If these multitudes of Christians have gone through persecutions, we must not think we can escape.

Choosing the cross involves daily discipline. It begins when we set our alarm clocks a little earlier to have a devotional time with God (see Chapter 4). It takes discipline to spend time in prayer, to do consistent Bible study, and to memorize Scripture. It takes discipline to go out regularly on personal evangelism. You cannot separate a disciple from discipline.

A Life Spent in Following Christ

One of the constant calls Jesus made to people was, "Follow Me!" (see Matthew 4:19; 8:22; Mark 2:14; 10:21; Luke 9:23; 14:27; John 1:43; 12:26; 21:22.) And one of the major characteristics of His life that we must follow was His complete obedience to His heavenly Father. He never varied from this. At the end of His life we find Him praying in His high priestly prayer, "I have brought You glory on earth by completing the work You gave Me to do" (John 17:4).

If we are to be disciples of Jesus Christ, our lives must be lived constantly in complete submission to the Father's will. Every facet of Christ's life must become the pattern for our lives as His disciples. Our lives must be spent completely and totally doing the will of God.

The Bible plainly reveals most of the will of God to us.

We are to carry out the commands to us in the Scripture, particularly as expressed in the declarative statements of the epistles of the New Testament.

We know that a Christian should pray; we know that a Christian should love; we know that a Christian should share his faith with others. But when it comes to our personal lives, knowing God's will takes a little more effort and prayer. It takes more thought, counsel, looking at circumstances, searching the Scriptures, and stepping out in faith. But there is nothing more joyful or peaceful than to know we are in the center of God's will.

I have experienced that joy and peace in my own life. How did I know that God wanted me to go to the Navigator headquarters for training in 1955? I prayed about it and sought counsel, and God worked out the circumstances so that there was not a doubt in my mind or heart when I was discharged from the Navy that this was His will for me. Later God clearly led my wife and me to Jacksonville, Florida. He then led us to Japan for four years and then to San Antonio, Texas. I am convinced now that it is His will for me to be on the staff of Coral Ridge Presbyterian Church, because as I spend time consistently in His Word, He confirms this to my soul.

A Fervent Love for All Who Belong to Christ

We are not only to love Jesus Christ supremely, but also to love one another with a fervent love. "A new commandment I give you," Jesus declared. "Love one another. As I have loved you, so you must love one another. All men will know that you are My disciples if you love one another" (John 13:34-35).

We read in 1 Corinthians 13 that this love considers others better than ourselves; it is willing to sacrifice. It is kind and patient. It does not delight in evil, but in truth.

141

Francis Schaeffer calls this love *the mark of the Christian*.[7] Without this love for the brethren, our discipleship is cold, sterile, and legalistic. Fervent love is an integral part of Christian discipleship for all who belong to Christ.

An Unswerving Commitment to the Scriptures

Jesus said, "If you hold to My teaching, you are really My disciples. Then you will know the truth, and the truth will set you free" (John 8:31-32). To hold to Jesus' teachings, we must constantly be in the Word of God—taking it in and digesting it. We deliberately take time to hear it, read it, study it, memorize it. We meditate on what we have taken in, applying these truths to our lives (see Chapter 3). This gives God the opportunity to speak to us regularly. We must see truth clearly in His Word, take inventory of our lives, and put that truth into practice. This is what James meant when he said, "Do not merely listen to the Word and so deceive yourselves. Do what it says" (James 1:22).

Many people attend church and hear fine preaching and teaching, but their lives do not change. Their hearing is not mixed with faith and obedience.

A Forsaking of All to Follow Christ

This is perhaps the most difficult and unpopular of all the terms of discipleship. But to be Christ's disciples, we must forsake all and follow Him. Jesus said, "Any of you who does not give up everything he has cannot be My disciple" (Luke 14:33). Many preachers avoid talking about this subject. Other preachers try to water down or rationalize what Jesus said. But His statement is clear: if we do not forsake everything, we *cannot* be His disciples.

This spirit is exemplified in the life of C. T. Studd, a British missionary to Africa. Studd had inherited a great deal of wealth, but "decided to give his entire fortune to Christ, and to take the golden opportunity offered him of doing what the rich young man failed to do . . . It was simple obedience to the [clear] statements of God's Word."[8]

He gave away thousands of pounds to the work of the Lord in England and overseas missions, but he saved the equivalent of about $9,600 for the woman he was about to marry. She was not to be outdone by her future husband's forsaking all to follow Jesus.

"'Charlie,' she asked, 'what did the Lord tell the rich young man to do?'

"'Sell all,' he replied.

"'Well then, we will start clear with the Lord at our wedding.' And off went that money also to Christian missions."[9]

That kind of spirit also characterized the life of Jim Elliot, one of five American missionaries killed by the Auca Indians in Ecuador in 1956. He wrote in his journal:

> Father, let me be weak that I might loose my clutch on everything temporal. My life, my reputation, my possessions, Lord, let me loose the tension of the grasping hand. Even, Father, would I lose the love of *fondling*. How often I have released a grasp only to retain what I prized by "harmless" longing, the fondling touch. Rather, open my hand to receive the nail of Calvary, as Christ's was opened—that I, releasing all, might be released, unleashed from all that binds me now. He thought heaven, yea, equality with God, not a thing to be clutched at. So let me release my grasp.[10]

Jesus Christ did not say that we must be *willing* to forsake all to follow Him, but that we *must* forsake all. In our affluent culture that is hard to do. No wonder churches across America are full of dead wood—people who have refused the way of discipleship and have chosen instead the road to mediocrity. Their lives are unfruitful and full of problems; they stagnate in their pews. They do not reflect the reality of the kind of life Jesus is talking about.

Whether you are a month old in the Lord, or six months, or a year, or much older, this passage and others like it must constantly confront us with Jesus' claims to our total allegiance. Many years ago, when I told the Lord, "You've got everything!" I meant it. I've had many struggles since then, and many times I have to tell the Lord I meant what I said. I want to be a disciple of the Lord Jesus Christ more than anything else, so I make sure I make that recommitment daily.

At the end of my life I would like the Lord to say to me, "Well done, good and faithful servant." The only way I'll hear that from Him is if I have forsaken all to follow Him. I either hold all things in the palms of my hands held out to Jesus, or I hold them in my fists, grasping them for all they are worth.

THE PRACTICAL APPLICATION OF DISCIPLESHIP

The Navigators place much emphasis on making disciples. My work with this organization has honed my thinking and my study of the Scriptures on this vital subject. Examining the teaching of the Bible and the ministry God has given us, we have come up with what we call a "Profile of a Disciple."

These ten basic guidelines provide an opportunity for personal evaluation by each one of us: "Am I a disciple?" They also give us a checkup system for our ministries: "Am I making disciples?" If I'm assisting someone in spiritual growth, these guidelines give me a plan to follow in his development.

These guidelines are for you to evaluate your own life and see what qualities you need to work on to be a functioning disciple of the Lord Jesus. Ask God to minister to your heart through His Holy Spirit, and to enable you to see how well you match these biblical criteria. Honest evaluation will help you to make an effort to add these ingredients to your life, with God's help.

A Disciple Puts Christ First in His Life, and Is Taking Steps to Separate from Sin

God wants us to place Jesus Christ first in our lives and submit to Him (see Chapter 6). You might ask God, "Lord, are You first in *all* areas of my life?" If He by His Holy Spirit reveals an area not under His control, we must confess that to Him. We must then purpose to make Jesus Christ Lord of our entire lives, and follow, obey, trust, and love Him.

When a person has been born again, he will evidence a sensitivity to sin. Old habits may cling to us and vie for attention and fulfillment, but with the Holy Spirit we can be victorious over sin. Paul wrote, "Sin shall not be your master, because you are not under the law, but under grace" (Romans 6:14). He also stated to Titus, "The grace of God that brings salvation has appeared to all men. It teaches us to say 'No' to ungodliness and worldly passions, and to live self-controlled, upright, and godly lives in this present age" (Titus 2:11-12). A disciple will seek to live a godly, pure life.

We cannot say we love God and continue to practice sin. As we saturate our lives with God's Word (see Chapter 3), we learn how to live our lives so that they are pleasing to Him.

A Disciple Has a Consistent Daily Devotional Time and Is Developing in His Prayer Life.

A disciple spends time daily in God's Word and in prayer, developing communication with his Saviour (see Chapter 4). I thank God for those who taught me to take time daily to seek God's face. I learned as a young Christian to take my Bible and use a notebook and pen to record observations as God faithfully revealed what He had for me each day. After reading His Word, I prayed, expressing to God my appreciation, confession, or whatever related to what He had revealed to me. The circle of communion was completed, and I could go into the day with confidence that God was with me in all situations.

David said, "Let me hear Thy lovingkindness in the morning; for I trust in Thee; teach me the way in which I should walk; for to Thee I lift up my soul" (Psalm 143:8).

A Disciple Demonstrates Faithfulness and a Desire to Learn and Apply the Word of God Through Regular Bible Study, Scripture Memory, Reading, and Meditation on the Scriptures.

To apply the Word of God to our lives, we must saturate our hearts and minds with it. Paul said, "Let the word of Christ dwell in you richly as you teach and counsel one another with all wisdom, and as you sing psalms, hymns and spiritual songs with gratitude in your hearts to God" (Colossians 3:16).

The Bible study we did last month or last year is not sufficient for today. We must continue learning more of the Word of God each day. Only this consistent practice will carry us through the Christian life. Multitudes of Christians testify they studied God's Word or memorized verses at some time before something happened and they quit. But a disciple continues in God's Word.

A Disciple Manifests a Heart for Witnessing, Gives His Testimony Well, and Presents the Gospel Regularly with Increasing Skill.

Evangelism is the key to making disciples. We must communicate the Gospel intelligently and adequately. Scripture tells us: "Always be prepared to give an answer to everyone who asks you to give the reason for the hope that you have" (1 Peter 3:15).

On one occasion I traveled through North Carolina and Florida for special evangelism training meetings. at each session I gave out a questionnaire to determine the evangelistic skills of those present. I found that most of the participants had not witnessed to anyone in the past year, or led anyone to Christ. They lacked evangelistic ability, and were not skilled in communicating the story of their own conversion. But after many hours of training and practice they learned how to present the Gospel effectively, and to give their testimonies. They later led scores of men and women to the Lord.

It is easy to get Christians to do many things, but it is relatively difficult to get them to witness faithfully, and to be willing to train others to do the same. Waylon Moore, who has been involved in evangelism and follow-up most of his adult life, says about 95% of church members have not led a person to Christ.[11]

A Disciple Attends Church and Maintains Close Ties with Its Fellowship, Displaying Love and Unity.

Being an active member of a local church is a vital necessity for every person who has received Jesus Christ as Saviour and Lord (Chapter 5). The writer of Hebrews tells us, "Let us consider how we may spur one another on toward love and good deeds. Let us not give up meeting together, as some are in the habit of doing, but let us en-

147

courage one another—and all the more as you see the Day approaching (Hebrews 10:24-25).

I met a man once who professed to be a Christian, but neither he nor anyone in his family attended church regularly. They were "turned off" because of an experience in a former church which had caused him great pain and bitterness. But now his whole family was suffering because they were out of fellowship with other believers, missing out on the joy and blessing of the family of God, in which love and unity are key factors. Disciples must be involved in a local church, following the pattern of the Early Church (see Acts 2—6) and demonstrating love and unity in fellowship.

A Disciple Demonstrates a Servant Heart by a Sincere Interest in Helping Others.

The Apostle Paul tells us of a Christian family in Corinth who proved their interest in others: "You know that the household of Stephanas were the first converts in Achaia, and they have devoted themselves to the service of the saints" (1 Corinthians 16:15).

I've met many Christians who were real servants, and one of them was Lee Roscoe. Lee was always available to do anything I asked him. In fact, he showed true servanthood by doing things I never asked him to do. He was a true faithful servant.

When we serve others, we are following the example of Jesus. His life is summarized in this statement: "For even the Son of Man did not come to be served, but to serve, and to give His life a ransom for many" (Mark 10:45).

Leaders are leaders because they are the greater servants. The way up is down. The way to honor our Lord and Saviour is to serve. There is always room for one more servant.

A Disciple Is a Learner—Open and Teachable.

Some people really want to learn, but not to be taught. This attitude should not characterize a disciple of Jesus Christ. A true disciple is open to instruction, rebuke, and encouragement from his leaders and fellow believers. He realizes he doesn't have all the answers, and needs the knowledge, gifts, and experience of others in the body of Christ.

I have seen many persons fall by the wayside because they were not open to instruction. In Charleston, South Carolina, my wife and I had three single men and a single girl living in our home for training in Christian discipleship. Two of the trainees repeatedly evidenced an unteachable spirit. We finally asked them to move out because our entire ministry of making disciples was being hindered by their refusal to be open and teachable.

I've often reflected on the lives of these four people who lived in our home. One is a business leader, and has a rich ministry of making disciples in his community. Another is a successful pastor. The two who were unteachable, however, have not done much for the Lord. What a price to pay!

For further instruction in this area, a study of what the Book of Proverbs says about reproof and instruction would be greatly rewarding.

A Disciple Is Giving Regularly and Honoring God with His Finances.

Harvey Oslund, a friend of mine in Columbia, Maryland, has discipled many men who are serving Christ today as leaders and makers of disciples. One of Harvey's greatest strengths is giving. He was challenged from the Word of God to honor God with his finances when he first became a Christian. He made a pact with some fellow

Christians, and they set out to prove God's promises about our giving. God blessed them, so they have increased the percentage of their giving, and God has continued to bless them. The men Harvey has trained are just like him. They are some of the most generous people I've ever met.

You can start today by making a decision to give God the tithe, which is one-tenth of your total income. In addition, give offerings to the Lord beyond your tithe. Someone has said the tithe is the obedience gift while the offering is the love gift. When you give beyond your tithe, you are telling God you love Him.

Paul taught the Corinthian Christians, "Each man should give what he has decided in his heart to give, not reluctantly or under compulsion, for God loves a cheerful giver" (2 Corinthians 9:7). We should give to our church, to personal friends, to the poor, to missionary organizations, and to others in need. Jesus said, "Give to everyone who asks you" (Luke 6:30).

A Disciple Will Demonstrate the Fruit of the Spirit by an Attractive Relationship with Christ and His Fellowman.

Paul declared, "The fruit of the Spirit is love, joy, peace, patience, kindness, goodness, faithfulness, gentleness, and self-control. Against such things there is no law" (Galatians 5:22-23). These Christlike characteristics are the outward evidence of the indwelling Christ.

All of us know Christians we would like to know better, and from whom we would like to learn the secrets of their beautiful relationship with Christ. Their lives have a poise and beauty that is highly attractive. We especially see this sometimes in the lives of older, more mature Christians, whom God by His sovereign grace has molded and shaped through the crucible of life. To my wife,

Norma, and me, one of these is Lila Trotman, wife of the founder of The Navigators. Every time we are with her, these Christlike qualities of love, graciousness, kindness, and peace are clearly visible. Truly she is a woman fashioned by God

We also see these same qualities in the lives of some younger Christians. Many have spoken of the love, patience, and kindness of a friend, roommate, or classmate who poured out his life for them. The relationship that developed from this exposure was often the catalyst that brought them to Christian maturity.

This attractive relationship with Christ is also visible to those who are not Christians. When I was in high school, a group of teenagers had a quality of life that attracted me. I remember arguing with them about eternal life, and claiming that no one could know where he was going after death. Yet I could not deny the attractiveness of their lives. It was this attraction which finally made me want to receive Christ as my Saviour. All of us know someone with such an attractive relationship with Christ that his life is a living testimony to the faithfulness of God.

True Christian discipleship is sharing not only what we know but also what we are. We don't necessarily ask another Christian to know what we know, but *to be what we are*. Men and women are helped to become disciples by having others share their lives with them. The godly example, the disciplined children, all lived out before others are often used by God to create in the hearts of fellow Christians a desire to become the same.

A Disciple Is Seeking to Determine and Use His Spiritual Gift or Gifts.

Everyone has at least one gift necessary to function properly in a ministry of making disciples. Each of us does not have all the gifts, but God has enabled each of us to make a specific contribution to the body of Christ. This truth is central to the New Testament, particularly in Paul's teaching to the Romans and the Corinthians (Romans 12; 1 Corinthians 12—14; see also Ephesians 4).

God has said that every Christian has at least one spiritual gift for the benefit of the whole body of Christ. No one has all the gifts, all have at least one gift, and some have two or more. We are dependent on each other.

One of the problems in the Church today is the scriptural ignorance of many believers about this vital subject. Many Christians have no idea what their spiritual gift is, much less how to use it to benefit the entire body of Christ. Older Christians must help other believers discover, develop and use their particular gift or gifts.

In making disciples, we must help Christians learn to exercise their God-given gifts and abilities. For a simple presentation on this subject you may want to read *Disciples Are Made—Not Born* by Walt Henrichsen. He gives many helpful suggestions in the chapter "Gifts and Calling."[12]

As you seek to grow in Christ and become a functioning disciple, carefully study 1 Corinthians 12 and Romans 12 with an open heart, asking God to help you discover your gift or gifts. God wants us to know what He has given us. "Each one should use whatever spiritual gift he has received to serve others, faithfully administering God's grace in its various forms" (1 Peter 4:10).

Review the ten points of discipleship, and with a prayer for enlightenment and understanding ask God to reveal the areas in your life that need developing. With the help of the Holy Spirit, you can do that to God's glory. Nothing is a more beautiful response to the Saviour than your commitment to be His disciple!

NOTES: 1. William MacDonald, *True Discipleship* (Kansas City, Kansas: Walterick Publishers, 1962), page 5.

2. H. A. Evan Hopkins, quoted in *True Discipleship*, page 5.

3. Walter A. Henrichsen, *Disciples Are Made—Not Born* (Wheaton, Illinois: Victor Books, 1974), page 30.

4. The outline for this section, "The Terms of Discipleship," is taken from *True Discipleship*, pages 5-9.

5. Henry Martyn, quoted in *True Discipleship*, page 6.

6. *Foxe's Book of Martyrs* (Chicago: Moody Press; Old Tappan, New Jersey: Fleming H. Revell Company).

7. Francis Schaeffer, *The Mark of the Christian* (Downers Grove, Illinois: InterVarsity Press, 1970).

8. Norman Grubb, *C. T. Studd* (London: The Lutterworth Press, 1957), page 64.

9. *C. T. Studd*, page 64.

10. Elisabeth Elliot, *Shadow of the Almighty* (New York: Harper and Brothers, 1958), page 246.

11. Waylon E. Moore, *New Testament Follow-up* (Grand Rapids, Michigan: Wm. B. Eerdmans Publishing Company, 1963), page 19.

12. *Disciples Are Made—Not Born*, Chapter 10, pages 131-138.

CHAPTER

8

GOD'S PLAN FOR A COMMITTED DISCIPLE'S LIFE

If we are convinced of the content of the preceding seven chapters, what do we do about it? What happens next? Jonathan Edwards, a great 18th-century preacher in New England, said, "Resolved, that every man should live to the glory of God. Resolved second, that whether others do this or not, I will." We must now ask ourselves, *Is this the consuming drive of my life? Do I intend to live to the glory of God? Do I want my life to count for Jesus Christ?* The choice is up to us.

The Bible exhorts us, "Therefore let us leave the elementary teachings about Christ and go on to maturity. Let us not lay again the foundation of repentance from acts that lead to death, and of faith in God" (Hebrews 6:1). The primary gifts we receive from the Lord when we come to Him—repentance and faith—enable us to receive Him as Saviour and Lord. After that, the words "let us . . . go on to maturity" are important to us. God challenges all of us to grow and mature. We are called on to continue growing, developing, and maturing in our relationship with Jesus Christ.

Furthermore, God is looking for men and women through whom He can demonstrate His power and grace. An Old Testament prophet once said to a king, "The eyes of the Lord move to and fro throughout the earth that He may strongly support those whose heart is *completely* His" (2 Chronicles 16:9). God is looking for men and women who will believe Him, follow Him, and literally lay down their lives for Him. He's looking for those whose hearts are completely His, those who will say, "Lord, count on me. I am willing to be your man or your woman in this community, in this business, on this base, or on this campus. What do You want me to do?"

We need to remember that God wants us to have a fruitful life. He wants to use us and give each of us a ministry in the lives of other people. He wants us to enjoy the Christian life. If we choose *not* to live God's way, then—according to the Word of God—we will lose all the joy, victory, and blessing of a truly abundant Christian life—including helping others find Jesus Christ. God meant for all of us who know Him to be involved in reaching the world with the Gospel. So we must continue to grow in our relationship with the Lord. That's why at the end of his second letter, Peter admonishes us to "grow in the grace and knowledge of our Lord and Saviour Jesus Christ" (2 Peter 3:18). This growth is vitally important.

God has provided everything we need in two vital areas of our lives. Peter tells us that "His divine power has given us everything we need for life and godliness through our knowledge of Him who called us by His own glory and goodness" (2 Peter 1:3). Everything we need for living the abundant life and behaving in a godly manner has been given to us. The term *godliness* in its broadest sense means the whole character of our Christian life. God has provided everything necessary to keep our lives on display before other believers and the world as a testimony to the value of knowing Him.

Peter goes on, "Through these He has given us His very great and precious promises, so that through them you may participate in the divine nature and escape the corruption in the world caused by evil desires" (2 Peter 1:4). When we receive Christ, we receive Him on the basis of God's great and precious promises. God has said, in effect, "If you come to Me, I will cleanse you from your sins, I will purify you in the blood of Christ, I will make you a whole new creation, and I will give you eternal life with Me in heaven." In one form or another, God gave these promises to enable us to live here on earth the kind of lives that are pleasing to Him. We find these promises throughout Scripture. By claiming them, they empower us to live a divine life in this evil world.

Peter continues:

> For this very reason, make every effort to add to your faith goodness; and to goodness, knowledge; and to knowledge, self-control; and to self-control, perseverance; and to perseverance, godliness; and to godliness, brotherly kindness; and to brotherly kindness, love. For if you possess these qualities in increasing measure, they will keep you from being ineffective and unproductive in your knowledge of our Lord Jesus Christ. But if anyone does not have them, he is nearsighted and blind, and has forgotten that he has been cleansed from his past sins (2 Peter 1:5-9).

That's the whole issue in a nutshell—God has a plan for maturing His disciples. He has provided everything.

157

All we have to do is add these qualities to our faith. When we walk in His ways of discipleship, these promises, as well as the power and the enabling to live God's way, are ours. Paul says this a little differently: "In Christ all the fullness of the Deity lives in bodily form, and you have this fullness in Christ, who is the head over every power and authority" (Colossians 2:9-10).

THE POTENTIALS OF OUR LIVES

Our lives have three basic potentials—uselessness, mediocrity, or fruitfulness. During my years of ministry among college students, servicemen, and the church community, I have dealt with these three subjects many times. Young men and women have lived in my home for training—people who had established quiet times, were studying and memorizing Scripture, and who had a dynamic evangelistic ministry. Some of them are still active for the Lord, but others are not. What makes the difference? Ultimately it is the path we choose to follow. Three paths are open to us.

Uselessness

Before we become Christians, we are useless to the kingdom of God. Amazingly, some believers seem to go nowhere spiritually after they come to Christ. There is no growth, no forward movement, no progress in their Christian lives. They remain babes in Christ, useless to the Lord.

Mediocrity

Many other Christians seem to prefer mediocrity. They are satisfied just to be in church. Otherwise, they remain completely uninvolved. Our churches today are full of these "once-a-week Christians." They have just enough Bible knowledge mixed with disobedience to make them miserable. As a result, they have most of the problems and occupy most of the time in counseling situations.

Fruitfulnesss

Fruitfulness is the third potential we all have. God can take any person who is committed to Him and who chooses this road, and make him or her an effective and fruitful disciple. Jesus said, "This is to My Father's glory, that you bear much fruit, showing yourselves to be My disciples" (John 15:8).

We face these choices every day. Each one of us must ask ourselves: *Am I going to spin my wheels today, totally lose all 24 hours, and be half-hearted about everything, or am I going to be fruitful today?* The choice is ours. We are what we are today; we are living and working where we are today; and we are there today because of a series of choices we made in the past. Spiritually, every one of us has the potential of being fruitful—if we choose that route. We can choose today to spend time alone with God or to sleep in. We can say, "Lord, I want my life to count for You today," or we can do nothing.

(After reading this chapter and finishing this book open your Bible to Psalm 119 and look for six verses in that psalm that have the expression "with my [the whole] heart" or "with all my [the] heart." Write them out and see what God expects us to do with all our hearts. Then meditate on these verses and ask God to show you how they relate to your life.)

The New Testament's commentary on the life of David is that he was a wholehearted man. Paul, in one of his sermons, said that David "served God's purpose in his own generation" (Acts 13:36). Those words challenge me.

159

It can be that way for us—we can choose to serve our generation. When I reach the end of my life, I want to make sure that I have served my generation by the will of God, as David did.

God wants that kind of life for every person who follows Jesus Christ. The people He is using mightily today are those who have chosen the road of discipleship, which is the route to fruitfulness. They saw the teaching in God's Word, believed it, and started living God's way, and realized God's potential of fruitfulness in their lives.

GOD'S CLAIM ON OUR LIVES

Because God is God, He has a claim on our lives by virtue of creation, redemption, and lordship.

Creation

Because God is the Creator of everything, including man, He has a claim on all His creatures. Paul stated to the philosophical Athenians that "in Him we live and move and have our being" (Acts 17:28). This means that our total lives are completely from God's hands. He is the source of all we are and have. Because He is our Creator, He has a prior claim on our lives.

Redemption

More important for a Christian, however, is the fact that God has a claim on us because He has redeemed us. Paul stated, "Do you not know that your body is a temple of the Holy Spirit, who is in you, whom you have received from God? You are not your own; you were bought at a price. Therefore honor God with your body" (1 Corinthians 6:19-20). We don't belong to ourselves. Because He died to redeem us from sin, Jesus Christ has prior claim on us. This is the reason He wants commitment, submission, and loyalty from us. He owns us and wants us to serve Him. He wants us to be able to say sincerely, "Lord, from today on my life is all Yours. I want You to use it any way You want."

Later, as we begin growing in discipleship and realizing our potential for fruitfulness, new choices confront us. Again we pray, "Lord, I want to make sure You know that as far as I am concerned, it's a hands-off policy on my life. It's all Yours. I want You to make me what You want me to be because You have infinite wisdom and love. I want You to change me to be like Jesus Christ, no matter what it takes." Every day we are faced with decisions of lordship and discipleship. We must constantly remember we are not our own; God has a prior claim on our lives because He has redeemed us from our sins.

Lordship

God also has a prior claim on our lives because He controls our lives—He is Lord (see Chapter 6). Remember that God is sovereign. Why do you think God has left us on earth after we received Jesus Christ as Saviour and Lord? Why didn't He immediately take us to heaven? One reason is that to be prepared for heaven, we need to grow and mature now. When we were born again, we were spiritual babies, and the rest of our lives on earth allows us to grow toward spiritual maturity. A second reason is that God has chosen Christians to be His instruments in getting the Gospel to the rest of the world.

As far as our position before God is concerned, the moment we trusted in Jesus Christ we were clothed with His righteousness (see Romans 1—8). God declared us righteous in Jesus Christ, and that position never changes.

161

But God left us in this world as His disciples to do the job of evangelizing the whole world.

Many Christians sitting in the pews of churches Sunday mornings have faced that crossroad and have chosen to go the route of noninvolvement and mediocrity. Yes, they know Jesus Christ as Saviour; they have eternal life. Once they faced some choices about following Him, but perhaps did not understand fully what they were, and chose to go in the wrong direction. As far as being used by God in evangelism, being in the army of Christ and having an impact on the world, they are out of the picture.

How different are they from their neighbors next door who do not know Jesus Christ? What evidence is there that they are Christians? Not too much. True, they go to a certain building for an hour or two Sunday mornings, but throughout the week their lives are not too much different from their non-Christian neighbors.

Many Christians find themselves in this position—some through ignorance but most through choice. They do not submit to the lordship of Christ, who as the sovereign King of the universe has every right to exercise that lordship. These people have perhaps heard the claims of discipleship presented, but have said, "That's not for me," and have chosen the path to mediocrity.

WHAT IS GOD'S PLAN FOR US?

The Bible reveals to us God's plan for His disciples. The Old Testament shows what God expects of His people, Jesus taught His disciples what He wanted them to do, and the epistles of the New Testament expound in great detail the responsibilities of Christian disciples. Let us look at six major categories regarding God's plan for us

We Are to Know Him

Knowing God is the most important category and is the basis for all the others. The most important thing we as Christians can do is to get to know the God who redeemed us from our sins. Christianity is primarily a relationship. When we received Jesus Christ as our Saviour and Lord, we were brought into a relationship with Him. At the heart of this relationship is the biblical fact that the Saviour and the redeemed sinner have been united—they have become one. In theology this is called the mystical union; the believer is now *in Christ*.

Even though we have a relationship with Jesus Christ, we need to realize that no relationship can grow or develop unless vital and meaningful communication exists. A man and a woman may marry, but if there is no communication between them, their relationship will not grow and develop. The same principle applies to us as Christians. We need to develop a growing relationship with Jesus Christ by continually communicating with Him.

We see this pattern in the life of the Apostle Paul. He first came to Christ at the crossroad of his life, on the road to Damascus. There, after Christ had spoken to his heart, Paul asked two questions: "Who are You, Lord?" (Acts 22:8) and "What shall I do, Lord?" (Acts 22:10). He spent the rest of his life putting the answers to these two questions into practice—getting to know Jesus Christ and doing His will. It cannot be emphasized too strongly that these two questions and their answers should also be a pattern for our lives. We should be committed to getting to know Jesus Christ and doing what He wants us to do.

Paul shares this great desire of his heart with us: "That I may gain Christ and be found in Him, not having a righteousness of my own that comes from the law, but that which is through faith in Christ—the righteousness that

163

comes from God and is by faith. *I want to know Christ* and the power of His resurrection and the fellowship of sharing in His sufferings, becoming like Him in His death" (Philippians 3:8-10). Earlier Paul had stated, "For it has been granted to you on behalf of Christ not only to believe on Him, but also to suffer for Him" (Philippians 1:29).

Paul's testimony should be the attitude of our hearts: "I want to know Him!" Paul spent his whole life getting to know Jesus Christ. Will that be the testimony of your life? How well do you know Him? Are you getting to know Him better every day? You should be, for Christ lives in you. Paul said the heart of Christianity is "Christ in you, the hope of glory" (Colossians 1:27). That means that when our lives are over and we are with Jesus Christ in heaven, we will be sharing His glory with Him. Meanwhile, we need to get to know Him.

We get to know Jesus Christ through His Word. "These are the Scriptures that testify about Me," Jesus said (John 5:39). God wants us to seek His face and His heart, and He wants to reveal His presence to us on a daily basis, but we must first seek Him (see Chapter 4). We open our Bibles and begin reading, and then talk to God in prayer. We say, "Lord, I know this is Your Word, and I know You want to talk to my heart. Help me to see You today in the pages of Your Book."

We Are to Experience God's Plan by Faith and Obedience

Not only do we first come to Christ by faith, but we must also live by faith. Paul, quoting from the Prophet Habakkuk, said, "The righteous will live by faith" (Romans 1:17; Habakkuk 2:4). Our daily lives should be characterized by a walk of faith. We see examples of this portrayed in the Great Hall of Fame in Hebrews 11. Here is a record of men and women of God who lived by faith throughout the history of the Old Testament. Their united testimony was that they believed God and walked in His ways. Faith is the key to victory and blessing in the Christian life.

When God brought us into His family and into a vital relationship with Jesus Christ, He gave us access to the plan He has for us. Nothing can give us greater confidence and peace of heart than to know we are in the will of God.

The writer to the Hebrews, after presenting the Great Hall of Fame of faith, made this important statement: "Therefore, since we are surrounded by such a great cloud of witnesses, let us throw off everything that hinders and the sin that so easily entangles, and let us run with perseverance the race marked out for us" (Hebrews 12:1).

The "heroes of the faith" and many others are the "cloud of witnesses" to which the writer referred. The emphasis was on the size of the testimony. Thousands of believers throughout the centuries have followed the plan of God for their lives—the race marked out for them.

This great cloud of witnesses unanimously testifies to the perfection of the plan God has for His people's lives. He has a plan that is just right for each of us. How important it is, then, for us to fall in step with that plan. This is how we can best invest our lives.

God has shown us a way to get the most from our lives in Psalm 90. It is the only psalm written by Moses, the servant of God, the great leader of Israel some 3,500 years ago. It could be titled "How to Invest Your Life," and contains eight principles on this vital subject. We want to look here at three of them.

We need to accept the fact that God is sovereign. Moses began with a prayer of adoration: "Lord, Thou hast been our dwelling place in all generations. Before the mountains were born, or Thou didst give birth to the earth and the world, even from everlasting to everlasting, *Thou art God"* (Psalm 90:1-2). That last brief phrase is Moses' acknowledgment of the Godhood of God—His sovereignty. Throughout the Scriptures, we are constantly confronted with the fact that God is God, and that He ordains the ways of men. Many passages show that men may plan their own ways but that God is ultimately in control.

Not only is God sovereign over our lives, but He is also sovereign over every single thing that enters our lives. Nothing happens by accident or without God's knowledge. Why does He permit such things as illness, tragedies, and testings to come into our lives? To build our faith, to demonstrate to us that He loves us, and to mold us into the kind of people He wants us to be. He has a plan for each of our lives, a plan that is absolutely best for us, and He wants to realize that plan in us. Peter said, "Dear friends, do not be surprised at the painful trial you are suffering, as though something strange were happening to you. But rejoice that you participate in the sufferings of Christ, so that you may be overjoyed when His glory is revealed" (1 Peter 4:12-13).

It is hard for us to accept suffering, for we are rebels at heart, always wanting to do "our own thing." But God is absolutely and completely sovereign over our lives. When we learn to accept this, everything else falls into place.

We need to realize the fact that life is brief. Moses vividly describes the brevity of our lives on earth:

> For a thousand years in Thy sight are like yesterday when it passes by, or as a watch in the night. Thou hast swept them away like a flood, they fall asleep; in the morning they are like grass which sprouts anew. In the morning it flourishes, and sprouts anew; towards evening

GOD'S PLAN FOR A COMMITTED DISCIPLE'S LIFE

it fades, and withers away . . . Thou has placed our iniquities before Thee, our secret sins in the light of Thy presence. For all our days have declined in Thy fury; we have finished our years like a sigh (Psalm 90:4-6, 8-9).

The older we get the more we realize how short life is. In our 20s and 30s, we don't think much about this; but when we get into our 40s and 50s, we begin to realize life is coming to an end. James asks us, "What is your life?" and answers, "You are a mist that appears for a little while and then vanishes" (James 4:14). You can go out on a cold morning, see your breath blow out in a mist, and watch it vanish rapidly away. That's how short our lives are in light of eternity. Someone has said:

Only one life, and it will pass;
Only what's done for Christ will last.

Only two things in this world are going to last into eternity—the Word of God and the souls of men. Everything else will be destroyed. "The day of the Lord will come like a thief. The heavens will disappear with a roar; the elements will be destroyed by fire, and the earth and everything in it will be laid bare" (2 Peter 3:10).

In light of this fact, how should we spend our lives? We should be doing eternal things. Moses said, "As for the days of our life, they contain seventy years, or if due to strength, eighty years, yet their pride is but labor and sorrow; for soon it is gone and we fly away. Who understands the power of Thine anger, and Thy fury, according to the fear that is due Thee?" (Psalm 90:10-11). What was Moses saying? He said everyone faces the same problems in life—the same financial reverses, the same tragedies of death, the same crippling diseases, the same misunderstandings. The man outside of Christ faces them just like the man in Christ does.

As Christians, however, we have an added dimension that unbelievers do not have. We have the Holy Spirit living in us, giving us the grace and enabling necessary to deal with the problems and pressures of life. Through these problems and pressures, God slowly transforms us into the kind of people He wants us to be. God can do so much with the short life of a Christian, if it is only given over to Him.

We need to take constant inventory of our lives. Moses said, "So teach us to number our days, that we may present to Thee a heart of wisdom" (Psalm 90:12). Throughout the Book of Proverbs, Solomon tells us that getting to know God is the wisest thing we can do. As we realize the shortness of our lives, and as we get to know God through His Word during each precious day He has given us, we can take inventory of our lives by comparing them to the teachings of Scripture.

David expressed this thought when he prayed, "Lord, make me to know my end, and what is the extent of my days, let me know how transient I am" (Psalm 39:4). We need to recognize the short amount of time left to us, and then live biblically according to God's plan. We need to live every day as though it were our last. Then we can face God with our heads held high, knowing we have done His will.

Solomon tells us that "the fear of the Lord is the beginning of wisdom" (Proverbs 9:10). Getting to know God and learning to reverence (fear) Him according to His plan is the wisest thing we can do. "Wisdom is the principal thing," Solomon says. "Therefore get wisdom, and with all thy getting get understanding" (Proverbs 4:7, KJV). For a valuable exercise, read through the Book of Proverbs, looking for the words *wisdom* and *wise*. Write the references down, and meditate on what each verse has to say to you about wisdom.

We Are to Be Transformed into the Image of Christ

A third part of God's plan for our lives is that we be transformed into the image of Jesus Christ. Paul states it clearly: "We know that in all things God works for the good of those who love Him, who have been called according to His purpose. For those God foreknew He also predestined *to be conformed to the likeness of His Son*, that He might be the firstborn among many brothers." (Romans 8:28-29).

From the first day we became Christians, God placed us in a training program to make us like His Son. Using His Word and prayer, He trains us through the deepening relationship we have with Christ in our devotional times, and slowly makes us more Christlike.[1] He is producing the quality of life in us that will bring the greatest amount of glory to Him.

God also uses circumstances that come into our lives, and His Word enables us to cope with them. When we respond biblically, we become more like Christ. The circumstances we face vary from individual to individual and from time to time. Let us consider some of them:

God uses financial pressures. Many of us face real financial stress at times. Unemployment, costly accidents, unexpected expenses, and many other situations test us. With each crisis, we again have the opportunity to believe that God is the provider of all we need. Or do we worry and try our own solutions? Here again, we need to recognize God's sovereignty over our lives and trust Him to provide financially in His way and in His time.

God uses our parents and families. Much of my

counseling is with teenagers and young adults. Some of it involves divorce situations where the children have rebelled against their parents or against God's principles rearding marriage. They have messed up their lives through reactions against what has happened in their parents' marriages. Often these family problems bring them to Christ. In the same way, Christians who do not surrender all to the lordship of Christ may also have family problems. They, too, need to learn to leave everything in the hands of a loving, sovereign God, and solve their marital and family problems biblically.

God also uses sickness, accidents, and the loss of loved ones to mold our characters. He uses misunderstandings by others, innuendos, attacks on our motives and persons, rebuke and chastisement to conform us to the image of Christ. The Bible says, "No discipline seems pleasant at the time, but painful. Later on, however, it produces a harvest of righteousness and peace for those who have been trained by it" (Hebrews 12:11). His discipline is hard, but the result is fulfilling.

God uses all these things and others to mold us into Christ's image. The key is how to respond to them. I have a little plaque on my wall written in old English script by a Chinese from Singapore, which contains someone's personal paraphrase of Romans 8:28: "The Lord may not have planned that this should overtake me, but He has most certainly permitted it. Therefore, though it were an attack of any enemy, it has the Lord's permission and therefore all is well. He will make it work together with all life's experiences for good." There are times when I look at that plaque and say, "Thank you, Lord." God uses these circumstances and pressures to transform us into the image of Jesus Christ, and we should be grateful that His love and concern is so comprehensive.

We Are to Take Our Places in the Body of Christ and Exercise Our Gifts

Another plan God has for our lives is that we be active members of His church, using the spiritual gifts He has given us. Remember that every believer has at least one spiritual gift; many have more than one. These gifts are the special enabling given to Christians by the Holy Spirit for their responsibilities in the body of Christ. They are given sovereignly and are to be used for edifying the other members of the body. (The gifts are listed in Romans 12:6-8, 1 Corinthians 12:4-11, 27-31, and Ephesians 4:11-12.)

Every Christian has the responsibility to discover his or her gifts and to exercise them for the benefit of the body of Christ. How do we discover our gifts? Here are some guidelines.

1. Get involved with people. Since spiritual gifts have been given to benefit other members of the body of Christ, we need to get involved with people. The gifts are never to be used selfishly for ourselves, but are to minister to and with other believers.

2. Realize that your gifts lie generally in the areas of your interests and are what you can most easily do. If you are uncomfortable or do not like doing something, in all probability that is not your gift. The Holy Spirit enables us to enjoy using our gifts.

3. Find people who can give you an honest evaluation of your possible gifts. Others will know whether you are ministering to them, and whether you are being fruitful through the exercise of that particular gift.

4. Ask for help in exercising your gift. For example, if you feel your gift is teaching, ask for opportunities to teach. This will help you discover whether this is your gift.

5. Distinguish between gifts and God-given respon-

sibilities. Not having a specific gift does not absolve you from your responsibility in areas in which God commands obedience. You may not have the gift of giving, but you are commanded to give to the Lord; you may not have the gift of faith, but you are required to exercise faith in God. You may not have the gift of evangelism, but you are commanded to be a witness.

We Are to Be Fruitful and Reproduce as Christians

A fifth thing God wants us to do in His plan is to be fruitful and to reproduce our lives in others. God wants every Christian to be a reproducer. One of the most valuable little booklets on this subject is *Born to Reproduce* by Dawson Trotman, founder of The Navigators.[2] It is a classic message on this biblical principle of spiritual reproduction.

The parable of the weeds. After Jesus had given the parable of the weeds, His disciples came to Him and said, "Explain to us the parable of the weeds in the field." He answered them, "The field is the world, and the good seed stands for the sons of the kingdom. The weeds are the sons of the evil one, and the enemy who sows them is the devil. The harvest is the end of the age, and the harvesters are angels" (Matthew 13:36-39).

The point we need to understand here is that the good seed represents us—the sons of the kingdom, Christian disciples, men and women who know Jesus Christ personally. Seed stored in a warehouse produces nothing. It becomes valuable and fruitful only when it is sown in plowed ground, is fertilized and watered, and eventually produces a harvest. A seed has life within itself and the power to reproduce. One kernel of corn sown into prepared soil produces many ears of corn, each containing hundreds of kernels.

Let's relate that principle to another that Jesus gave us: "I tell you the truth, unless a kernel of wheat falls to the ground and dies, it remains only a single seed. But if it dies, it produces many seeds" (John 12:24). Good spiritual seed is life-giving. It must be sown in the field of the world by Jesus Christ. It has the power to reproduce, but in order to do so it must die.

How does this apply to us? We must die to self and to living our own way. We have to commit ourselves to doing things according to the plan God has laid out for us. Then we will reproduce spiritually a hundredfold or more. This is the law of reproduction and the promise of Scripture.

Seed has no control over itself and cannot demand its own way. It is sown wherever the sower wants to sow it. Likewise, we need to be totally available to the Lord, our Sower, to be used in His field, the world. We must be willing to be sown wherever He wants to plant us.

Several years ago, a young Christian sailor was transferred from San Francisco to Charleston, South Carolina, where I was ministering with The Navigators. He was assigned to a minesweeper which had a crew of about 36 men—a good field for spreading the Gospel. But one night after we had spent some time together I discovered that he was living ashore in an apartment with another sailor. At the end of our evening together I asked him, "Do you believe that God in His sovereignty and in His direction over yur life had you transferred from San Francisco to Charleston?"

Without hesitation, he replied, "You bet! No question about it."

I asked, "Do you believe that God placed you on that minesweeper?"

"Yes, no question about it."

"Do you believe that God put you on that mine-sweeper so that you as a Christian might influence some of the other men on that ship?"

"I'm sure of it."

"Well, do you believe that even though there may be only a handful of men left on that ship at night, God wants you to seek out and reach those six or eight men?"

"No question about it," he replied.

"Then why are you living in that apartment?"

Within a few days, he moved back aboard ship. Do you see what had happened? He had been like a seed trying to run his own life. Little feet had suddenly grown on that seed and taken him where *he* wanted to go. God had placed him on that ship and wanted him aboard even if there were only six or eight men there at times. That's the principle of the seed being available to God.

God has placed me in the ministry He wants me to have. He has placed you where He wants you to be. And we are called on to reproduce in the fields where God has placed us. It could be in your church, in the office or shop where you work, in the apartment building or neighborhood where you live, or in your school. Wherever God has placed you, wherever you have been sown, that's where you must die to self and reproduce for Him. That's the plan of God; that's the way of Scripture.

Three barriers to fruitfulness. Three things will keep us from being fruitful, both spiritually and physically:

1. Immaturity. Children cannot bear babies; they are immature. New babies need to be nurtured. An immature Christian also cannot reproduce, but spiritually it does not take as long as it does physically.

2. Sterility or other impairment to reproduction. There are many physical conditions which impair reproduction, but the major spiritual impairment is sin. If

we are living with unconfessed sin in our lives, we will be spiritually sterile and cannot be fruitful and reproduce.

3. Lack of union. Physically, an intimate relationship between husband and wife is necessary for reproduction. Spiritually, this is represented by our ongoing relationship with the Lord. That is why we have stressed in this book the vital importance of our daily relationship with Jesus Christ.

We Are to Help Fulfill the Great Commission

A final principle in the plan of God for our lives is that He wants us involved in personal evangelism. He wants us to help fulfill the Great Commission. His orders were for us to "go into all the world and preach the Good News to all creation" (Mark 16:15).

This commission is the great divider of Christians. Many fail to follow God's plan for them in this area. The result is mediocrity. They may have been growing well, but when faced with the responsibility of sharing their faith with others, they take the path of least resistance, choosing noninvolvement. Instead of facing this command biblically, believing that God can help them in this area as well, they choose to ignore God's mandate. This decision affects the rest of their lives. It is tragic that many Christians are not willing to do their part in carrying out the Great Commission.

Jesus stated, "Go and make disciples!" (Matthew 28:19) That command applies to every Christian in every generation. It's our God-given responsibility, and one day we must answer God's question, "What did you do to help fulfill My Great Commission?" Jesus wants to say to each of us, "Well done, good and faithful servant!" (Matthew 25:21, 23) The Great Commission is the Continental Divide between those who choose to live their lives according to God's plan and those who want to go their own way, living for themselves alone.

A final word of challenge: Jesus said, "Salt is good, but if it loses its saltiness, how can it be made salty again? It is fit neither for the soil nor for the manure pile; it is thrown out. He who has ears to hear, let him hear" (Luke 14:34-35). What Jesus is saying is that a Christian who refuses to take his place as a disciple of the Lord and get involved in the Great Commission, is just as useless as a lump of salt that is no longer salty. To avoid becoming useless for God, get involved in helping fulfill the Great Commission. God's blessing is on all those who do.

CONCLUSION

It has been almost 2,000 years since Jesus commissioned His small band to go and make disciples in all the world. The original group grew into a mighty force as Christianity spread throughout the earth. Everywhere these disciples went they carried the message of the Gospel. As men and women responded to it they in turn were trained and became disciples, and took the message elsewhere.

Then came the Dark Ages. Christianity degenerated to ritual, ceremony, and observances which watered down the cutting edge of biblical discipleship. Yet throughout history there has always been a remnant—men and women who stood firm and fought for the purity of the Gospel and the faith. Their faith exemplified the biblical commitment to true discipleship.

Since the birth of the modern missionary movement in the late 1700s, we have seen the return of an emphasis on biblical discipleship carrying out the Great Commission. More books about this topic are being written by competent and experienced authors; Christian colleges offer courses in which students are confronted with the biblical teachings on discipleship. This book was written with the desire that God would use it to clarify and bring into focus the necessary elements of Christian discipleship.

Why not ask God to give you a heart to be His disciple? Giving your life to a ministry of making disciples is the most rewarding and productive thing any Christian can do. This reproductive ministry has the greatest long-range potential of fulfilling the Great Commission. No other Christian activity can replace it. The Apostle Paul was motivated by this great challenge and expressed it this way: "For what is our hope, our joy, or the crown in which we will glory in the presence of our Lord Jesus when He comes? Is it not you? Indeed, you are our glory and joy" (1 Thessalonians 2:19-20). Jesus also said, "If anyone would come after Me, he must deny himself and take up his cross and follow Me. For whoever wants to save his life will lose it, but whoever loses his life for Me and for the Gospel will save it" (Mark 8:34-35).

Study the Word of God so you will know what is involved in discipling others. Be prepared to discover that it is costly. Yet the rewards far outstrip the expenses as you realize that God has used you to help another Christian become what God intended him or her to be.

Why not ask God to give you such a ministry? As you pray, begin to look around you for those who would respond to the challenge—in your church, youth group, men's group, women's group, and your neighborhood. Most of all, remember that those you personally lead to Christ are prime sources for such a ministry.

In the midst of your busy life, you can be discipling at least one other person. May the promises of Isaiah be yours to claim:

If you give yourself to the hungry, and satisfy the desire of the afflicted, then your light will rise in darkness, and your gloom will become like midday. And the Lord will continually guide you, and satisfy your desire in scorched places, and give strength to your bones; and you will be like a watered garden, and like a spring of water whose waters do not fail. And those from among you will rebuild the ancient ruins; you will raise up the age-old foundations; and you will be called the repairer of the breach, the restorer of the streets in which to dwell (Isaiah 58:10-12).

God also promised, "The smallest one will become a clan, and the least one a mighty nation. I, the Lord, will hasten it in its time" (Isaiah 60:22).

I thank God for those whom He used to pick me up as a young Christian and to help me grow and mature in Christ. They were men who shared their lives with me; they were men and women whose vision and dedication lit a flame in my heart for the Lord.

Only eternity will tell the numerous lives that can be touched by *yours*, as you, by God's grace and power, walk in submission to Christ, ministering His Gospel to others.

NOTES: 1. A booklet that will help you toward becoming like Jesus Christ is *Christlikeness* by Jim White (NavPress, 1976).
2. *Born to Reproduce* by Dawson Trotman (NavPress, 1975) is a classic booklet on this subject.

SCRIPTURE INDEX